D0119145

Betty Crocker's
Cake Decorating
with Cake Recipes for Every Occasion

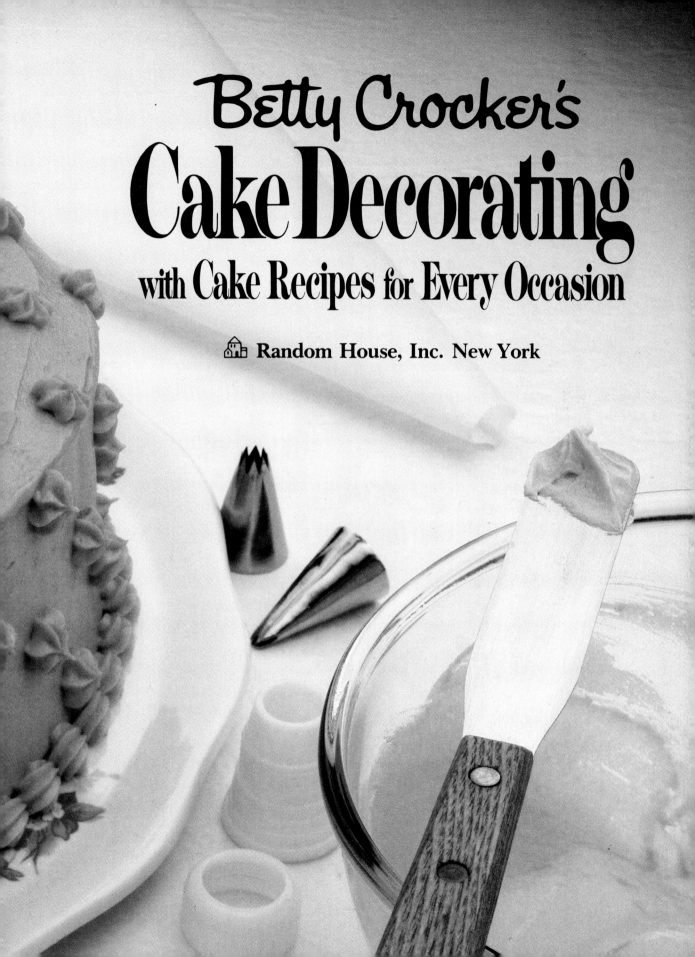

Betty Crocker's
Cake Decorating
with Cake Recipes for Every Occasion

Random House, Inc. New York

Cake decorating is a universally appealing subject, and few cooks are more admired than those who create the glorious cakes with which we celebrate the memorable occasions and honor the special people in our lives. *Betty Crocker's Cake Decorating Book* takes cake decorating out of the "professionals only" category and enables anyone to bake delicious cakes and to frost and decorate them with a creative flourish. In these pages, the Betty Crocker Kitchens experts lead the novice with many color photographs, how-to sketches and explicit directions through every step of baking and decorating beautiful cakes for friends and family.

So if you have always wished that you could bake and decorate cakes, begin today. Here are more than one hundred of Betty Crocker's very best, tested cake recipes and as many delicious frostings, fillings and glazes. All of these cakes have been photographed in color to help you duplicate them exactly. The cake recipes are for such basic favorites as chocolate, spice and butterscotch as well as for angel foods and chiffons, sponge and pound cakes, cake rolls and cupcakes. Recipes offer time-saving cake and frosting mix substitutions wherever appropriate.

For those who consider a decorating bag and tips unfathomable mysteries, there is a section with how-to sketches for efficiently and confidently making a variety of borders, simple designs and lovely flowers. There are also sketches on how to prepare cakes for decorating, including removing layers from pans, splitting layers easily and storing cakes correctly. Additional hints for successful cake decorating appear throughout the book.

Included are many other fast, simple decorating ideas requiring no special equipment — like Gumdrop Cats, Frosted Cranberries and Orange Peel Tulips. There are roses made from tinted frosting, chocolate, a lemon or gumdrops — even directions for sugaring a real rose as an elegant addition to an angel food cake.

Follow the easy-to-understand recipes, study the *how-to* sketches and be inspired by the *new* and *different* decorating ideas. Then let your imagination carry you on to creative fun and success with beautiful cakes you bake and decorate yourself. Best of all, bask in the admiration this new skill will win you.

Betty Crocker

Copyright © 1984 by General Mills, Inc., Minneapolis, Minnesota

All rights reserved under International and Pan-American Copyright Conventions. Published in the United States by Random House, Inc., New York and simultaneously in Canada by Random House of Canada Limited, Toronto.

Library of Congress Cataloging in Publication Data
Crocker, Betty. Betty Crocker's Cake Decorating with Cake Recipes for Every Occasion.

Includes index 1. Cake. 2. Cake Decorating. I. Title. II. Title: Cake Decorating with Cake Recipes for Every Occasion.
TX771.C723   1984   641.8'653   83-43202   ISBN 0-394-53591-X

Manufactured in the United States of America   24689753   First Edition

Contents

Introduction

The equipment, tips and techniques described here are your guide to the best and easiest ways to bake, frost and decorate your beautiful special occasion cakes. Practice will give you confidence and assure you of successful results every time.

Important: All cake and frosting recipes in this book were carefully tested. In the process of this testing, we used portable as well as standard mixers since surveys show that the majority of mixers in use in the United States are the portable type. Standard mixers are usually more powerful than portables so, for the initial step of beating layer cake ingredients until blended, reduce the speed of the standard mixer to low to prevent splattering.

Decorating Basics

1. It is important that the frosting to be used for decorating is the right consistency. Borders and drop flowers can have a medium consistency frosting, roses and other flowers need a firmer frosting so the petals will hold their shape and frosting to be used for writing, leaves and simple line designs can be slightly thinner.

2. Powdered sugar must be completely free of lumps when it is to be used for a decorating frosting. If there are even small lumps it will be necessary to sift it.

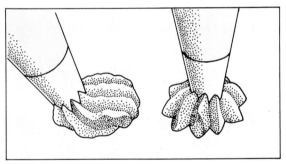

3. Most designs are made by holding the decorating bag at a 45° angle as shown above. For drop flowers, stars, dots and rosettes, hold the bag at a 90° angle (perpendicular to the surface).

4. Before piping a design or a message on a cake, lightly outline the design with a wooden pick to use as a guide. Short strips of sewing thread can be lightly placed on the frosted cake to mark the position of the message.

5. Use steady pressure to press out the frosting. The amount of pressure will determine the size and evenness of any design. To finish a design, stop the pressure and lift the point up and away.

6. When adding food color, remember that frosting will darken slightly as it sets. For vivid or deeper food colors, use paste food color.

7. A turntable or lazy Susan is a helpful tool to make it easier and faster to frost and decorate cakes.

Decorating Bags

Decorating bags used for cake decorating include the reuseable plastic-coated decorating bag or the disposable parchment paper or plastic bags. The plastic-coated decorating bag can be used with or without a coupler. The coupler saves time by enabling you to change decorating tips while still using the same bag of frosting. A coupler is not used for large decorating tips.

Here are step-by-step directions for using the decorating bags. (If you have a cake decorating set, it will include directions for assembly and use.)

How to Fit Your New Decorating Bag with a Coupler

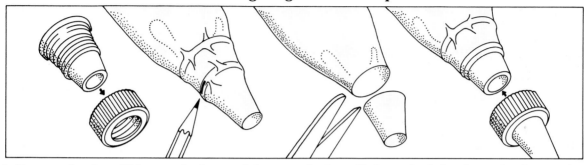

1. Unscrew the ring off the coupler base and drop the base, narrow end first, down into the end of the bag. Push the coupler base as far down into the bag as possible.

2. With a pencil, mark the location of the coupler's bottom thread on the outside of the bag. Push the coupler up and out of the bag.

3. Cut off the end of the decorating bag at the pencil mark. (Be careful not to cut too much; you can always trim a little more later if necessary.)

4. Replace the coupler base in the bag, pushing it down so the 2 bottom threads of the coupler show through the open end of the bag. Place decorating tip in ring and screw onto coupler base.

How to Use Your Decorating Bag

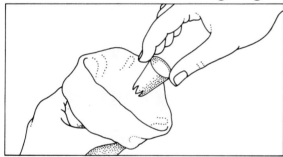

1. If not using a coupler or if the decorating tip is large, simply place the tip in the bag. If using a coupler, place the desired decorating tip on the coupler base and screw the coupler ring into place over the tip to hold it securely. With tip in place you're ready to fill the bag with frosting.

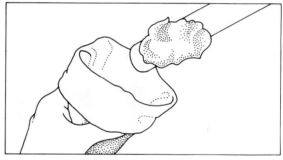

2. To fill the bag with frosting or whipped cream, fold down the open end of the bag to form a cuff approximately 2 inches wide. Hold the bag beneath the cuff and, using a spatula, fill the bag half full with frosting. (It is important not to fill the bag too full as the extra frosting will back up out of the bag.)

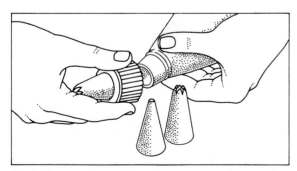

3. To change decorating tips, unscrew the coupler ring, remove the tip, replace it with another tip and screw the ring on again.

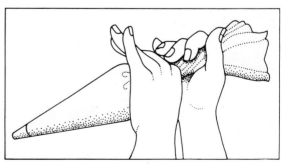

4. To close the bag, unfold the cuff and twist the top of the bag, forcing the frosting down into the tip. Continue to twist end of bag as you decorate.

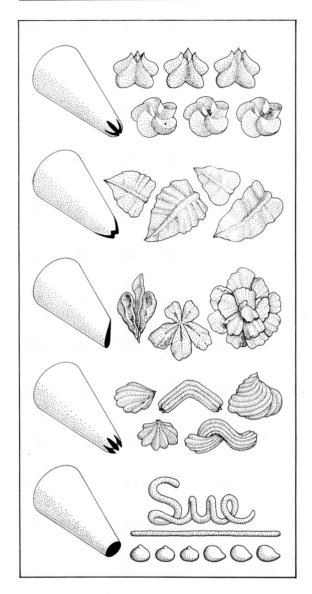

Decorating Tips and Their Uses

Drop Flower Tips: These tips make the easiest flowers for a beginning cake decorator. They are made directly on the frosted cake. The number of petals is determined by the number of openings in the end of the tip. Drop flower tips can be used to make either plain or swirled drop flowers. Popular drop flower tips include numbers 107, 129, 190, 217, 224, 225, 1C, and 2D.

Leaf Tips: The V-shaped opening of this tip forms the pointed end of the leaf. Leaf tips make plain, ruffled or stand-up leaves. Leaf tips can also be used to make attractive borders. Popular leaf tips include 65, 67 and 352.

Petal Tips: These tips are used for making roses, wild roses, violets, sweet peas and carnations. They are also used for making ribbons, bows, swags and ruffles. Popular petal tips include numbers 101, 102, 103 and 104. For very large roses, number 127 can be used.

Star Tips: These tips are used for making shell, rope and zigzag borders, stars, rosettes and can also be used for making drop flowers. Popular star tips include numbers 13 through 22 and can range in size from small to very large. Large star tips include numbers 32, 43 and 8B

Writing Tips: Writing tips are also called plain or round tips. In addition to writing messages, these tips can be used for making beads, dots, balls, stems, vines and flower centers. Popular writing tips include numbers 1 through 4 (small), 5 through 12 (medium) and 1A and 2A (large).

How to Make Rosettes and Drop Flowers

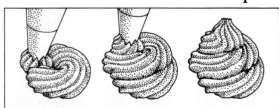

Rosettes: Using a star tip, press out whipped cream or frosting, using steady, even pressure, into a circle. Then, without stopping, spiral the whipped cream on top in a smaller circle, finally ending the swirl in a peak as you decrease the pressure.

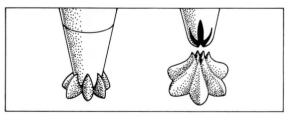

Drop Flowers: Using a drop flower tip, hold the decorating bag perpendicular (straight up) with the tip touching surface. Squeeze the bag, keeping the tip in frosting until petals are formed. Stop pressure and pull away.

Borders

Shell Border: As the name implies, this is a series of shells connected in a continuous line. Using a star tip, hold decorating bag at a 45° angle to surface. Press out frosting using consistent heavy pressure to create a full base. Raise the tip as shell builds up. Decrease pressure, drawing frosting to a point. Begin the next shell directly over that point.

Reverse Shell Border: This border is similar to the plain Shell Border except that as the shell is built up, circle to the right and decrease pressure. The second shell is circled to the left. Continue, alternating shells from right to left.

Bead Border: This technique is the same as the Shell Border technique except uses a writing tip. Vary pressure to make different size balls.

Zigzag Border: Using a star or writing tip, hold the decorating bag at a 45° angle to surface. Press out frosting with a steady, even pressure, moving bag from side to side slightly to form a zigzag line.

Rope Border: Using a star or large writing tip, hold the decorating bag at a 45° angle to the surface. Touch the tip to the surface and squeeze the bag, moving the tip down, up and around to the right, forming a slight "s" curve. Stop pressure and pull the tip away. Place the tip under bottom curve of the first "s" and repeat the procedure. Continue joining "s" curves to form rope.

Swag Border: Using a star, petal or writing tip, hold the decorating bag at a 45° angle to the surface. As you press out frosting, move the tip down and up, down and up as if writing a continuous letter "U". Use steady, even pressure as you repeat the procedure. When completed, discontinue pressure and pull the tip away.

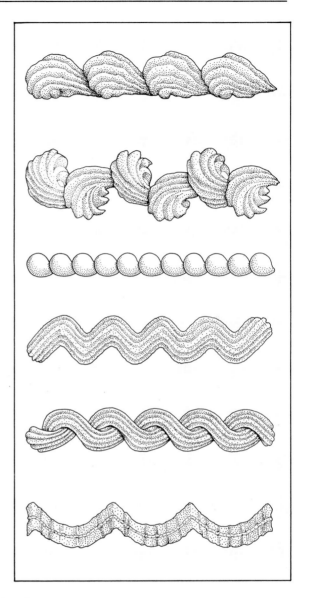

How to Make Basic Leaf and Simple Designs

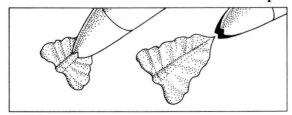

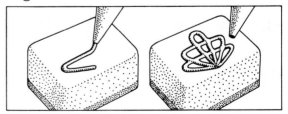

Basic Leaf: Using a leaf tip, hold the decorating bag at an angle to the surface. Squeeze and hold tip in place to let the frosting fan out to form base of leaf. Decrease pressure as you slowly pull the tip away and lift slightly to draw the leaf to a point.

Simple Designs: Using a writing tip, hold the decorating bag at a 45° angle. With the tip raised slightly from the surface squeeze the bag, applying pressure evenly, and direct the tip to outline the desired design. To end the design stop squeezing, touch tip to surface and pull away.

How to Use a Flower Nail

The flower nail is used to make flowers such as roses and marigolds. The frosting used to make flowers on a flower nail should be quite stiff.

To use a flower nail, attach a 2-inch square of waxed paper to the nail with a small dab of frosting. Hold the stem of the nail between the left thumb and forefinger and slowly rotate the nail to the left (counterclockwise). Hold the decorating bag in the right hand and press out frosting to form the petals. (Left-handed decorators should reverse these directions.)

Flowers can be made in advance and air dried or they can be placed directly on the cake.

How to Make Marigolds

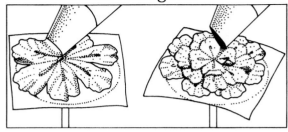

1. Touch the wide end of petal tip to center of flower nail, lifting narrow end slightly. Pipe a circle of narrow petals, each about ½ inch long, using a continuous back and forth motion. Turn the nail slowly as you pipe.

2. Pipe 2 or 3 more rows of petals, one on top of the other, making the petals in each row shorter than the last.

How to Make Roses

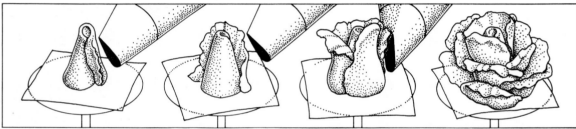

1. Using a petal tip, hold the bag with narrow end of the tip up. Turn the flower nail counterclockwise and press out frosting in a tiny circle to form center of rose.

2. To form the first petal, make a standing half circle to one side of center.

3. Add 2 more petals, forming a triangle.

4. Add more petals, overlapping, until rose is desired size. Remove the waxed paper with rose from the nail. Place on a level surface and let stand until set. Carefully lift the rose from waxed paper with a spatula and place on the cake. Attach with additional frosting if necessary.

NOTE: For very large roses, use tip #127.

How to Make Wild Roses or Apple Blossoms

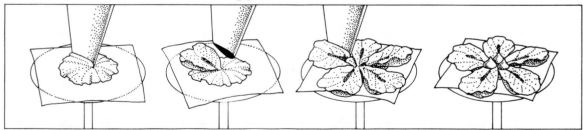

1. Make a small flat circle of frosting in center of flower nail for base of flower (petals are to be connected securely to this).

2. Using a petal tip, hold the bag with wide end of tip touching center of nail and narrow end almost parallel to nail's surface. As you press out the first petal, turn the nail to the left and move the tip out to the edge of nail and back to center. Stop pressure at center to complete petal and move tip away.

3. Make 4 more petals the same way, always working to the right of the previous petal.

4. Change to a writing tip and hold the bag perpendicular (straight up) to the center of the flower. Press out 2 or 3 small dots at center.

Measuring Ingredients

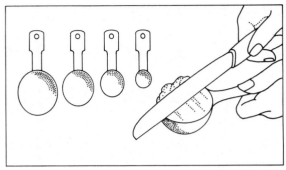

Use graduated nested measuring cups for measuring nonliquids. For all-purpose flour and granulated sugar, dip the cup into the ingredient to fill, then level. (Do not sift flour to measure or to combine with other ingredients.)

For cake flour and powdered sugar, lightly spoon into the cup, then level. (Sift powdered sugar only if it is lumpy — if it is sifted the quantity may need to be increased.)

Graduated spoons are used to measure thin liquids. Pour the liquid into the appropriate spoon until full.

For dry ingredients and thick liquids, pour or scoop into the appropriate spoon until full, then level with a straight-edged knife or spatula. If your set of spoons does not have a ⅛ teaspoon measure, use the ¼ teaspoon, fill it and remove half.

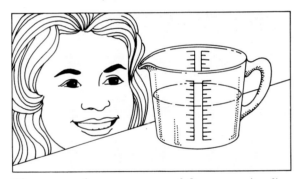

Glass measuring cups are used for measuring liquids. Read the measurement at eye level.

Spoon brown sugar and shortening into the cup, then pack down firmly. For nuts, coconut and cut-up or small fruit, lightly spoon into the cup, then pack down lightly.

Removing Layer Cakes from Pans

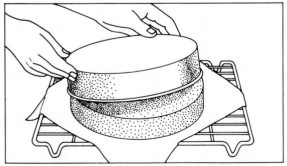

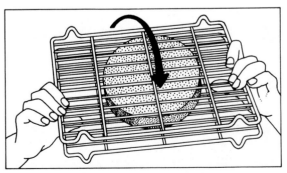

Cool the cake layers in pans on wire racks 10 minutes. Cover one rack with a towel; place towel side down on top of layer; invert as a unit. Remove pan.

Place a rack on bottom of layer; turn over both racks so the layer is right side up. Repeat with other layer(s). Allow layers to cool completely on racks.

Splitting Layer Cakes

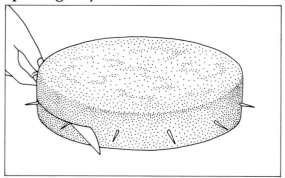

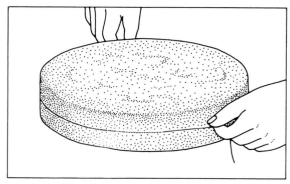

Wooden pick markers: Mark middle points on sides of layer with wooden picks. Using picks as a guide, cut through the layer with long, thin sharp knife.

Thread trick: Split the layer by pulling a piece of heavy sewing thread horizontally, back and forth, through the layer.

Frosting Layer Cakes

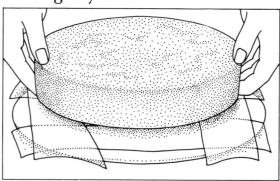

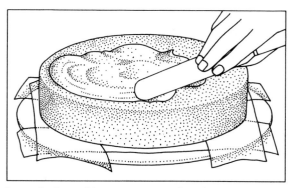

Place 4 strips of waxed paper around the edge of cake plate. Brush away any loose crumbs from the cooled cake layer. Place the layer on a plate, rounded side down. (The waxed paper will protect the plate as you frost and can be removed later.)

Spread about ⅓ cup creamy frosting (½ cup if fluffy frosting) over the top of the first layer to within about ¼ inch of the edge.

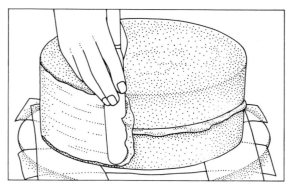

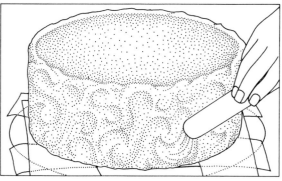

Place the second layer, rounded side up, on the first layer so that the 2 flat sides of the layers are together with frosting in between. Coat the side of the cake with a very thin layer of frosting to seal in the crumbs.

Frost the side of the cake in swirls, making a rim about ¼ inch high above the top of the cake to prevent the top from appearing sloped. Spread the remaining frosting on top, just to the built-up rim.

Cooling and Removing Angel Food and Chiffon Cakes from Pan

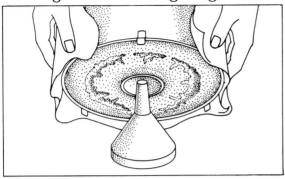

Invert the pan on a heatproof funnel or bottle and let hang until cake is cold.

Loosen the cake by moving a spatula or table knife up and down against side of pan.

Splitting Angel Food and Chiffon Cakes into Layers

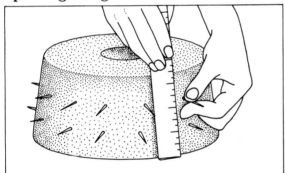

Measure the cake with a ruler and mark into 3 equal widths with wooden picks. Using a serrated knife and with wooden picks as a guide, cut across

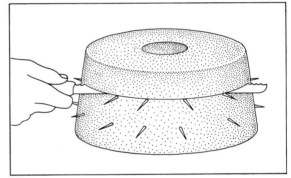

the cake with a light, sawing motion. The same technique can be used for splitting into 4 layers.

Use of Dowels

If you wish, dowels or legs can be added to large tiered cakes for support and stability. Dowels should be about ⅛ inch higher than each tier. Insert the dowel through tier to plate or cardboard round. Use 4 to 8 dowels per tier, depending on the size of the layer.

Arrange the dowels in a circle, square or rectangle slightly smaller than the tier placed directly on top of them. Place the next tier on cardboard round on top of dowels. Repeat with remaining tiers except the top tier. Dowels can be of wood or plastic. If using separators or columns, refer to the manufacturer's directions.

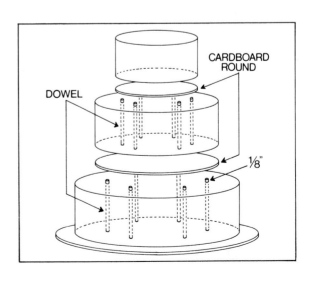

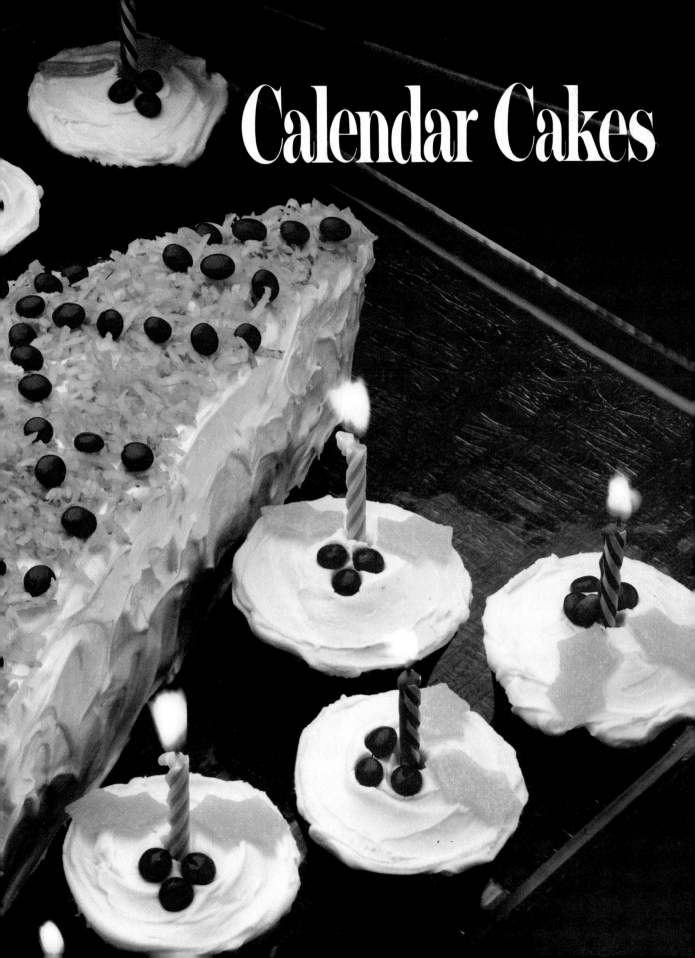

Calendar Cakes

Christmas Tree Cake

Starlight Cake (below)
White Mountain Frosting
(right)
Green food color

1 cup flaked coconut
2 peppermint candy canes
Red cinnamon candies

Bake Starlight Cake as directed. Prepare White Mountain Frosting; tint pale green with 5 or 6 drops food color. Cut cake as shown in diagram. Arrange cake pieces 1 and 2 on large tray or aluminum foil-covered cardboard; frost. Place piece 3 on top; frost sides and top, making strokes through frosting to resemble tree branches.

Shake coconut and 2 to 4 drops green food color in tightly covered jar until coconut is evenly tinted; sprinkle on cake. Insert peppermint candy canes into end of tree to make trunk. Place red cinnamon candies on tree to form garlands. 12 to 16 servings.

Starlight Cake

2 cups all-purpose flour
1½ cups sugar
½ cup shortening (half
margarine or butter,
softened, if desired)
1 cup milk

3½ teaspoons baking
powder
1 teaspoon salt
1 teaspoon vanilla
3 eggs

Heat oven to 350°. Grease and flour rectangular pan, 13 × 9 × 2 inches. Beat all ingredients in large bowl on medium speed, scraping bowl constantly, until blended, about 30 seconds. Beat on high speed, scraping bowl occasionally, 3 minutes. Pour into pan.

Bake until wooden pick inserted in center comes out clean, 40 to 45 minutes. Cool 10 minutes; remove from pan. Cool completely.

White Mountain Frosting

½ cup sugar
¼ cup light corn syrup
2 tablespoons water

2 egg whites
1 teaspoon vanilla

Mix sugar, corn syrup and water in 1-quart saucepan. Cover and heat to rolling boil over medium heat. Uncover and boil rapidly until candy thermometer registers 242° or until small amount of mixture dropped into very cold water forms a firm ball that holds its shape until pressed.

As mixture boils, beat egg whites in small bowl just until stiff peaks form. Pour hot syrup very slowly in a thin stream into egg whites, beating constantly on medium speed. Add vanilla; beat on high speed until stiff peaks form.

NOTE: To get an accurate temperature reading on the thermometer, it may be necessary to tilt the saucepan slightly. It takes 4 to 8 minutes for the syrup to reach 242°. Preparing this type of frosting on a humid day can require a longer beating time.

○ *Time-saver Tip:* Substitute 1 package (18.5 ounces) yellow cake mix with pudding for the Starlight Cake. Prepare and bake as directed on package. Substitute 1 package (7.2 ounces) fluffy white frosting mix for the White Mountain Frosting. Prepare as directed on package.

Cutting and Assembling Christmas Tree Cake

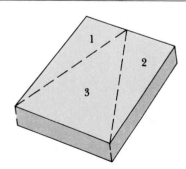

Cut cake diagonally into 3 pieces.

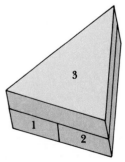

Arrange side pieces on tray; frost top. Place remaining piece on top; frost sides and top.

Pictured on preceding page: Christmas Tree Cake, (above), center, Gumdrop Holly Cupcakes, (page 17) top and bottom

Gumdrop Holly Cupcakes

Cardamom Cupcakes
 (below)
Creamy Cardamom
 Frosting (below)

Large green gumdrops
Red cinnamon candies
Small red or green candles,
 if desired

Bake Cardamom Cupcakes as directed. Frost with Creamy Cardamom Frosting. Roll green gumdrops, one at a time, on heavily sugared board until ⅛ inch thick. Cut to resemble holly leaves. Arrange 2 or 3 leaves on each cupcake; add 2 or 3 red cinnamon candies for holly berries. Insert candle in center of each cupcake. 3 dozen cupcakes.

Cardamom Cupcakes

2 cups all-purpose flour	3½ teaspoons baking
1½ cups sugar	powder
½ cup shortening (half	1 teaspoon salt
margarine or butter,	¼ teaspoon ground
softened, if desired)	cardamom
1 cup milk	1 teaspoon vanilla
	3 eggs

Heat oven to 350°. Beat all ingredients in large bowl on medium speed, scraping bowl constantly, until blended, about 30 seconds. Beat on high speed, scraping bowl occasionally, 3 minutes. Pour into paper-lined medium muffin cups, 2½ × 1¼ inches, filling each about half full.

Bake 20 minutes. Immediately remove from pan. Cool completely.

Creamy Cardamom Frosting

3 cups powdered sugar	⅛ teaspoon ground
⅓ cup margarine or	cardamom
butter, softened	2 tablespoons milk
1 teaspoon vanilla	

Beat all ingredients on medium speed until smooth and spreading consistency. If necessary, stir in additional milk, ½ teaspoon at a time.

○ *Time-saver Tip:* Substitute 1 package (18.5 ounces) yellow cake mix with pudding for the Cardamom Cupcakes. Prepare and bake as directed on package for cupcakes except add ¼ teaspoon ground cardamom before beating. Substitute 1 package (7.2 ounces) creamy white frosting mix for the Creamy Cardamom Frosting. Prepare as directed on package except add ⅛ teaspoon ground cardamom before beating.

Holiday Eggnog Cake

Eggnog Cake (below)
Eggnog Fluff (below)

3 tablespoons orange
 marmalade
Red and green food
 color

Bake Eggnog Cake as directed. Fill layers and frost cake with Eggnog Fluff. Mark 3 bells on top of cake with bell-shaped cookie cutter. Mix 2 tablespoons of the marmalade and 1 or 2 drops green food color. Mix remaining marmalade and 2 or 3 drops red food color. Fill 2 bells with green marmalade and 1 bell with red marmalade. Dip wooden pick into additional green food color and draw lines to connect bells. Refrigerate any remaining cake. 12 to 16 servings.

Eggnog Cake

2 cups all-purpose flour	1 teaspoon salt
1½ cups sugar	1 teaspoon ground
½ cup shortening (half	nutmeg
margarine or butter,	¼ teaspoon ground
softened, if desired)	ginger
1 cup milk	1 teaspoon rum
3½ teaspoons baking	flavoring
powder	3 eggs

Heat oven to 350°. Grease and flour 2 square pans, 8 × 8 × 2 inches, or 2 round pans, 8 or 9 × 1½ inches. Beat all ingredients in large bowl on medium speed, scraping bowl constantly, until blended, 30 seconds. Beat on high speed, scraping bowl occasionally, 3 minutes. Pour into pans.

Bake until wooden pick inserted in center comes out clean, 30 to 35 minutes. Cool 10 minutes; remove from pans. Cool completely.

Eggnog Fluff

Beat 1½ cups chilled whipping cream, ½ cup powdered sugar and 1 teaspoon rum flavoring in chilled bowl until stiff.

○ *Time-saver Tip:* Substitute 1 package (18.5 ounces) yellow cake mix with pudding for the Eggnog Cake. Prepare and bake as directed on package except add 1 teaspoon ground nutmeg, ¼ teaspoon ground ginger and 1 teaspoon rum flavoring to mix before beating.

Chocolate Nesselrode Cake

Dark Chocolate Cake (below)	*¼ cup powdered sugar*
1 cup chilled whipping cream	*¼ cup Nesselrode**
	Cocoa Fluff (below)
	Cut-up candied fruit

Bake Dark Chocolate Cake as directed. Beat whipping cream and powdered sugar in chilled bowl until stiff. Fold in Nesselrode. Fill layers and frost top of cake with Nesselrode mixture. Frost side of cake with Cocoa Fluff. Arrange cut-up candied fruit on top of cake in a wreath design. Refrigerate any remaining cake. 12 to 16 servings.

*¼ cup cut-up candied fruit and 1 teaspoon rum flavoring can be substituted for the Nesselrode.

Dark Chocolate Cake

2 cups all-purpose flour or cake flour	*½ teaspoon baking powder*
2 cups sugar	*1 teaspoon vanilla*
½ cup shortening	*4 ounces melted unsweetened chocolate (cool)*
¾ cup water	
¾ cup buttermilk	
1 teaspoon baking soda	*2 eggs*
1 teaspoon salt	

Heat oven to 350°. Grease and flour 3 pans, 8 × 1½ inches. Beat all ingredients in large bowl on medium speed, scraping bowl constantly, until blended, 30 seconds. Beat on high speed, scraping bowl occasionally, 3 minutes. Pour into pans.

Bake until wooden pick inserted in center comes out clean, 30 to 35 minutes. Cool 10 minutes; remove from pans. Cool completely.

NOTE: Cake can be baked in two 9-inch round pans. When cool, split to make 4 layers (see page 12). Fill layers and frost top of cake with ¼ each of the Nesselrode mixture.

Cocoa Fluff

Beat 1 cup chilled whipping cream, ½ cup powdered sugar and ¼ cup cocoa in chilled bowl until stiff.

○ *Time-saver Tip:* Substitute 1 package (18.5 ounces) devils food cake mix with pudding for the Dark Chocolate Cake. Prepare and bake as directed on package for two 9-inch rounds. Split cake to make 4 layers (see page 12).

Clockwise from top: Holiday Eggnog Cake (page 17), Christmas Coconut Cake (page 20), Chocolate Nesselrode Cake

Christmas Coconut Cake

Coconut Cake
 (below)
Tutti-frutti Filling
 (right)

1½ cups chilled whipping
  cream
¼ cup powdered sugar
½ teaspoon almond
  extract

Bake Coconut Cake as directed. Fill layers and frost top of cake to within 1 inch of edge with Tutti-frutti Filling. Beat whipping cream, powdered sugar and almond extract in chilled bowl until stiff. Reserve 1½ cups whipped cream mixture for decorating; frost side of cake with remaining whipped cream. Place reserved whipped cream in decorating bag with large open star tip #4B. Pipe large whipped cream shells around top edge of cake. Refrigerate any remaining cake. 12 to 16 servings.

Coconut Cake

4 egg whites
½ cup sugar
2 cups plus 2
  tablespoons
  all-purpose flour
1 cup sugar

½ cup shortening
3½ teaspoons baking
  powder
1 teaspoon salt
1 cup milk
⅔ cup flaked coconut

Heat oven to 350°. Grease and flour 2 round pans, 9 × 1½ inches. Beat egg whites in large bowl until foamy. Beat in ½ cup sugar, about 1 tablespoon at a time; continue beating until stiff and glossy. Do not underbeat.

Beat flour, 1 cup sugar, the shortening, baking powder and salt in another large bowl on medium speed, scraping bowl constantly, until blended, about 30 seconds. Beat in milk on high speed, scraping bowl occasionally, 2 minutes. Fold batter and coconut into egg whites. Pour into pans.

Bake until wooden pick inserted in center comes out clean, 30 to 35 minutes. Cool 10 minutes; remove from pans. Cool completely.

Tutti-frutti Filling

2 egg yolks
⅔ cup dairy sour cream
⅔ cup sugar
1 cup finely chopped
  pecans

⅔ cup flaked coconut
1 cup finely chopped
  raisins
1 cup finely chopped
  candied cherries

Mix egg yolks and sour cream in saucepan; stir in sugar. Cook over low heat, stirring constantly, until mixture simmers and begins to thicken. Remove from heat; stir in pecans, coconut, raisins and cherries. Cool.

○ *Time-saver Tip:* Substitute 1 package (18.5 ounces) white cake mix with pudding for the Coconut Cake. Prepare and bake as directed on package except stir ⅔ cup flaked coconut into batter.

EGG TIPS

Eggs are available most often in these sizes: extra-large (27 to 29 ounces per dozen), large (24 to 26 ounces per dozen) and medium (21 to 23 ounces per dozen). Our cake recipes have been tested with large eggs. Two eggs equal ⅓ to ½ cup; 3 eggs, ½ to ⅔ cup; 4 eggs, ⅔ to 1 cup. Egg whites equal about 2 tablespoons each; yolks, 1½ tablespoons.

For better volume, let egg whites stand at room temperature about 15 minutes before beating. Beat whites in a clean, dry bowl with a clean beater. Any yolk or fat in the whites will prevent them from beating properly.

Leftover egg whites can be stored covered in the refrigerator 7 to 10 days. Leftover egg yolks should be covered with water and can be stored in a covered container in the refrigerator 2 to 3 days. To freeze whites, place in a plastic ice cube tray, then remove the frozen cubes to a plastic bag for storage. Thaw frozen whites in the refrigerator.

Many cake and frosting recipes call for egg whites only. Leftover yolks can be used in custards, scrambled eggs, boiled dressings, egg pastries and cake fillings. Recipes in this cookbook that call for egg yolks only include:

Tutti-frutti Filling (above)
Pineapple Cream Filling (page 121)
Dark Chocolate Filling (page 128)
Custard Cream Filling (page 132)
Chocolate-Almond Filling (page 108)
Orange-Lemon Filling (page 109)
Lemon Filling (page 116)
Chocolate Loaf Cake (page 77)

New Year's Eve Cake

Chocolate Mint Cake (below)
Fluffy Mint Frosting (right)
4 or 5 tablespoons powdered sugar
12 flat chocolate peppermint patties
Miniature chocolate chips or red cinnamon candies

Bake Chocolate Mint Cake as directed. Prepare Fluffy Mint Frosting; reserve ¼ cup for decorating. Fill and frost cake with remaining frosting. Stir enough powdered sugar into reserved frosting until desired consistency for writing. Place in decorating bag with writing tip #2; write numbers on patties. Place patties in circle around top edge of cake. Make hands of clock with chocolate chips. 12 to 16 servings.

Chocolate Mint Cake

1⅔ cups all-purpose flour or 2 cups cake flour
1½ cups sugar
⅔ cup cocoa
½ cup shortening
1½ cups buttermilk
1½ teaspoons baking soda
1 teaspoon salt
1 teaspoon vanilla
¼ teaspoon peppermint extract
2 eggs

Heat oven to 350°. Grease and flour 2 round pans, 9 × 1½ inches. Beat all ingredients in large bowl on medium speed, scraping bowl constantly, until blended, 30 seconds. Beat on high speed, scraping bowl occasionally, 3 minutes. Pour into pans.

Bake until wooden pick inserted in center comes out clean, 30 to 35 minutes. Cool 10 minutes; remove from pans. Cool completely.

Fluffy Mint Frosting

½ cup sugar
¼ cup light corn syrup
2 tablespoons water
2 egg whites
1 teaspoon vanilla
½ teaspoon peppermint extract
Green food color

Mix sugar, corn syrup and water in 1-quart saucepan. Cover and heat to rolling boil over medium heat. Uncover and boil rapidly until candy thermometer registers 242° or until small amount of mixture dropped into very cold water forms a firm ball that holds its shape until pressed.

As mixture boils, beat egg whites in small bowl just until stiff peaks form. Pour hot syrup very slowly in a thin stream into egg whites, beating constantly on medium speed. Add vanilla and peppermint extract; beat on high speed until stiff peaks form. Tint pale green with 4 or 5 drops food color.

New Year's Eve Cake

Cherry Brownie Cake

Cherry Brownie Cake

Milk Chocolate Brownie Cake (right)	*2 packages (7 ounces each) marzipan*
Cherry Fudge Frosting (right)	*Powdered sugar*
Red food color	*Black shoestring licorice*
	Buttercream Frosting (right)

Bake Milk Chocolate Brownie Cake as directed. Frost with Cherry Fudge Frosting. Mark frosting into 24 servings, 2½ inches square. Knead food color, 1 drop at a time, into marzipan until cherry red. Roll marzipan on surface lightly sprinkled with powdered sugar into roll, ¾ inch in diameter. Cut into ¾-inch pieces; roll pieces into balls.

Mark creases in cherries with back of knife. Place a cherry on each serving. Cut licorice into 1½-inch

pieces for stems. Place Buttercream Frosting in decorating bag with leaf tip #352. Pipe leaves onto each stem. 24 servings.

Milk Chocolate Brownie Cake

1 cup margarine or butter	*2 cups sugar*
1 cup water	*½ cup dairy sour cream*
⅓ cup cocoa	*1 teaspoon baking soda*
2 cups all-purpose flour	*½ teaspoon salt*
	2 eggs

Heat oven to 375°. Grease and flour jelly roll pan, 15½ × 10½ × 1 inch. Heat margarine, water and cocoa to boiling in 3-quart saucepan, stirring occasionally. Remove from heat. Stir in flour, sugar, sour cream, baking soda, salt and eggs; beat until smooth. (Batter will be very thin.) Pour into pan.

Bake until wooden pick inserted in center comes out clean, 20 to 25 minutes. Cool completely.

Cherry Fudge Frosting

1 package (6 ounces) semisweet chocolate chips	*3 cups powdered sugar*
	⅓ cup maraschino cherry juice
2 tablespoons margarine or butter	

Heat chocolate chips and margarine over low heat, stirring constantly, until chocolate is melted. Beat in powdered sugar and cherry juice until frosting is smooth and spreading consistency.

Buttercream Frosting

1 cup powdered sugar	*1 tablespoon milk*
2 tablespoons margarine or butter, softened	*⅛ teaspoon green food color*
2 tablespoons shortening	

Beat all ingredients except food color on medium speed until frosting is smooth and desired consistency. If necessary, stir in additional milk, ½ teaspoon at a time. Stir in food color.

○ *Time-saver Tip:* Substitute 1 package (18.5 ounces) milk chocolate or chocolate fudge cake mix with pudding for the Milk Chocolate Brownie Cake. Prepare and bake as directed on package. Substitute 1 package (14.3 ounces) milk chocolate frosting mix for the Cherry Fudge Frosting. Prepare as directed on package.

Miniature Logs

Cherry Chiffon Cupcakes
(below)

Chocolate Fudge Frosting
(right)
Gumdrop Hatchets (right)

Bake Cherry Chiffon Cupcakes as directed. Put 2 cupcakes together end-to-end with Chocolate Fudge Frosting as shown. Frost sides of logs; leave ends unfrosted. Make strokes in frosting with fork to resemble bark. Place a gumdrop hatchet on each log. 19 logs (38 cupcakes).

Cherry Chiffon Cupcakes

2¼ cups cake flour
1½ cups sugar
  3 teaspoons baking
    powder
  1 teaspoon salt
½ cup vegetable oil
  5 egg yolks
½ cup cold water
¼ cup maraschino
    cherry juice

  1 teaspoon vanilla
  1 cup egg whites
    (about 8)
½ teaspoon cream of
    tartar
½ cup finely chopped
    maraschino
    cherries, well
    drained

Heat oven to 400°. Mix flour, sugar, baking powder and salt. Beat in oil, egg yolks, water, cherry juice and vanilla with spoon until smooth. Beat egg whites and cream of tartar in large bowl until stiff peaks form.

Pour egg yolk mixture gradually over beaten egg whites, folding with rubber spatula just until blended. Sprinkle cherries over batter; fold in with a few strokes. Pour into paper-lined medium muffin cups, 2½ × 1¼ inches, filling each ¾ full.

Bake until top springs back when touched lightly, 12 to 14 minutes. Immediately remove from pan; cool completely.

Chocolate Fudge Frosting

  9 squares (1 ounce
    each) semisweet
    chocolate
1½ cups margarine or
    butter

3¾ cups powdered sugar
¾ cup half-and-half
½ teaspoon salt
1½ teaspoons vanilla

Heat chocolate and margarine in saucepan over low heat until melted. Stir in remaining ingredients; beat until smooth. Place pan of frosting in bowl of ice and water; continue beating until frosting is smooth and spreading consistency.

Gumdrop Hatchets

Roll large red gumdrops on well-sugared board into ⅛-inch ovals. Cut hatchets from ovals as shown in diagram.

Assembling Miniature Logs and Gumdrop Hatchet Preparation

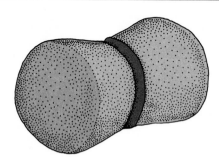
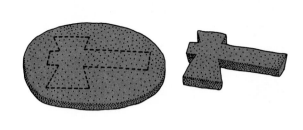

Put 2 cupcakes together with frosting.   **Cut** hatchets from rolled gumdrops.

George Washington Cake

Chocolate-Cherry Cake (below)	12 to 16 maraschino cherries with stems
Chocolate-Cherry Frosting (below)	

Bake Chocolate-Cherry Cake as directed. Reserve ¾ cup Chocolate-Cherry Frosting for decorating; fill layers and frost cake with remaining frosting. Place reserved frosting in decorating bag with star tip #32. Pipe border and lines on cake to form 12 to 16 wedges, applying even pressure and making side to side motion. Place a maraschino cherry on each wedge. 12 to 16 servings.

Chocolate-Cherry Cake

2 cups all-purpose flour or cake flour	1 teaspoon vanilla
2 cups sugar	½ teaspoon almond extract
½ cup shortening	4 ounces melted unsweetened chocolate (cool)
¾ cup water	
¾ cup buttermilk	
1 teaspoon baking soda	2 eggs
1 teaspoon salt	½ cup finely chopped maraschino cherries, well drained
½ teaspoon baking powder	

Heat oven to 350°. Grease and flour 2 round pans, 9 × 1½ inches, or 3 round pans, 8 × 1½ inches. Beat all ingredients in large bowl on medium speed, scraping bowl constantly, until blended, about 30 seconds. Beat on high speed, scraping bowl occasionally, 3 minutes. Pour into pans.

Bake until wooden pick inserted in center comes out clean, 30 to 40 minutes. Cool 10 minutes; remove from pans. Cool completely.

Chocolate-Cherry Frosting

4 cups powdered sugar	1 ounce melted unsweetened chocolate (cool)
½ cup margarine or butter, softened	
⅓ cup maraschino cherry juice	¼ teaspoon almond extract

Beat all ingredients on medium speed until smooth and desired consistency. If necessary, stir in additional cherry juice, ½ teaspoon at a time.

○ *Time-saver Tip:* Substitute 1 package (18.5 ounces) devils food cake mix for the Chocolate-Cherry Cake. Prepare and bake as directed on package except stir ½ cup well-drained, finely chopped maraschino cherries into batter.

Cherry Heart Cake

Cocoa Fudge Cake (below)	¼ teaspoon almond extract
1 cup chilled whipping cream	1 can (21 ounces) cherry pie filling
3 tablespoons powdered sugar	

Bake Cocoa Fudge Cake as directed. Beat whipping cream and powdered sugar in chilled bowl until stiff. Stir in almond extract.

Form narrow rim of whipped cream around top edge of bottom layer; spread about ⅔ of the pie filling on layer up to rim. Top with second layer. Outline large heart on top of cake with tip of knife. Frost side and top of cake, leaving heart portion unfrosted. Fill heart with remaining cherry filling. Refrigerate any remaining cake. 12 to 16 servings.

Cocoa Fudge Cake

1⅔ cups all-purpose flour or 2 cups cake flour	1½ cups buttermilk
	1½ teaspoons baking soda
1½ cups sugar	1 teaspoon salt
⅔ cup cocoa	1 teaspoon vanilla
½ cup shortening	2 eggs

Heat oven to 350°. Grease and flour 2 round pans, 9 × 1½ inches. Beat all ingredients in large bowl on medium speed, scraping bowl constantly, until blended, 30 seconds. Beat on high speed, scraping bowl occasionally, 3 minutes. Pour into pans.

Bake until wooden pick inserted in center comes out clean, 30 to 35 minutes. Cool 10 minutes; remove from pans. Cool completely.

○ *Time-saver Tip:* Substitute 1 package (18.5 ounces) chocolate fudge cake mix with pudding for the Cocoa Fudge Cake. Prepare and bake as directed on package.

Valentine Rose Cake

Silver White Cake (below)   *Gumdrop Rose (right)*
Pink Mountain Frosting
   (right)

Bake Silver White Cake as directed. Place square layer on large tray or aluminum foil-covered cardboard, 18 × 15 inches. Cut round layer into halves. Place cut edge of each half against adjacent sides of square layer to form heart as shown in diagram. Frost with Pink Mountain Frosting. Decorate with Gumdrop Rose. 10 to 14 servings.

Silver White Cake

2¼ cups all-purpose flour   3½ teaspoons
1⅔ cups sugar   baking powder
⅔ cup shortening   1 teaspoon salt
1¼ cups milk   1 teaspoon vanilla
                    5 egg whites

Heat oven to 350°. Grease and flour square pan, 8 × 8 × 2 inches, and round pan, 8 × 1½ inches. Beat flour, sugar, shortening, milk, baking powder, salt and vanilla in large bowl on medium speed, scraping bowl constantly, until blended, about 30 seconds. Beat on high speed, scraping bowl occasionally, 2 minutes. Beat in egg whites on high speed, scraping bowl occasionally, 2 minutes. Pour into pans.

Bake until wooden pick inserted in center comes out clean, 30 to 35 minutes. Cool 10 minutes; remove from pans. Cool completely.

Pink Mountain Frosting

½ cup sugar   2 egg whites
¼ cup light corn syrup   1 teaspoon vanilla
2 tablespoons water   8 drops red food color

Mix sugar, corn syrup and water in 1-quart saucepan. Cover and heat to rolling boil over medium heat. Uncover and boil rapidly until candy thermometer registers 242° or until small amount of mixture dropped into very cold water forms a firm ball that holds its shape until pressed.

As mixture boils, beat egg whites in small bowl just until stiff peaks form. Pour hot syrup very slowly in thin stream into egg whites, beating constantly on medium speed. Add vanilla and food color; beat on high speed until stiff peaks form.

Gumdrop Rose

Roll 4 large gumdrops on well-sugared board into ⅛-inch ovals as shown. Sprinkle with sugar. Cut ovals into halves. Roll one half-oval tightly to form center of rose. Place more half-ovals around center, overlapping slightly. Press together at base; trim base. Cut leaves from rolled out green gumdrops if desired.

○ *Time-saver Tip:* Substitute 1 package (18.5 ounces) white cake mix with pudding for the Silver White Cake. Prepare and bake as directed on package. Substitute 1 package (7.2 ounces) fluffy white frosting mix for the Pink Mountain Frosting. Prepare as directed on package except add 8 drops red food color.

Cutting and Assembling Valentine Rose Cake

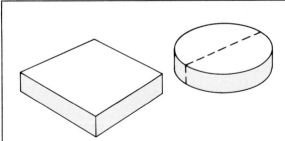

Cut round layer into halves.

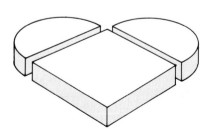

Place cut edges against sides of square layer.

Valentine Rose Cake, left, Cherry Heart Cake (page 25), right

Gumdrop Rose Preparation

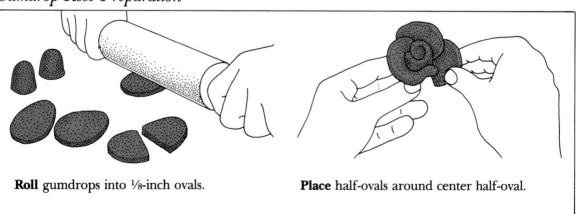

Roll gumdrops into ⅛-inch ovals.

Place half-ovals around center half-oval.

Easter Basket Cake

*Bonnie Butter Cake
(below)*
*Creamy Chocolate Frosting
(right)*

*1 cup shredded coconut
Green food color
Candy Easter eggs*

Bake Bonnie Butter Cake as directed. Fill layers and frost side of cake with Creamy Chocolate Frosting, bringing frosting up over edge of cake to form a rim about 1 inch wide. Spread thin layer of frosting on remaining top of cake. Make a basket weave pattern in frosting on side of cake by drawing inch-long horizontal and vertical lines with tines of fork.

Shake coconut and 3 or 4 drops green food color in tightly covered jar until coconut is evenly tinted; sprinkle on top of cake within rim. Place candy eggs on coconut. Make basket handle, if desired, by twisting pipe cleaners or wire; cover with aluminum foil, wind with ribbon and insert in sides of cake. 12 to 16 servings.

Bonnie Butter Cake

*1¾ cups sugar
⅔ cup margarine or
    butter, softened
1½ teaspoons vanilla
2 eggs*

*2¾ cups all-purpose flour
    or 3 cups cake flour
2½ teaspoons baking
    powder
1 teaspoon salt
1¼ cups milk*

Heat oven to 350°. Grease and flour 3 round pans, 8 × 1½ inches, or 2 round pans, 9 × 1½ inches. Beat sugar, margarine, vanilla and eggs in large bowl on medium speed, scraping bowl constantly, until blended, about 30 seconds. Beat on high speed, scraping bowl occasionally, 5 minutes. Beat in flour, baking powder and salt alternately with milk on low speed. Pour into pans.

Bake until wooden pick inserted in center comes out clean, 30 to 35 minutes. Cool 10 minutes; remove from pans. Cool completely.

Creamy Chocolate Frosting

*2½ cups powdered sugar
½ cup margarine or
    butter, softened*

*2 ounces melted
    unsweetened
    chocolate (cool)
1 teaspoon vanilla
2 tablespoons milk*

Beat all ingredients on medium speed until smooth and spreading consistency. If necessary, stir in additional milk, ½ teaspoon at a time.

○ *Time-saver Tip:* Substitute 1 package (18.5 ounces) yellow cake mix with pudding for the Bonnie Butter Cake. Prepare and bake as directed on package. Substitute 1 package (14.3 ounces) chocolate fudge frosting mix for the Creamy Chocolate Frosting. Prepare as directed on package.

CHOCOLATE TIPS

Chocolate can be melted in several ways:

1. Heat chocolate chips or squares uncovered in a heavy saucepan over low heat, stirring occasionally, until melted.

2. Microwave ½ to 1 cup chocolate chips uncovered on medium (50%) 3 to 4½ minutes, 1 or 2 squares 3 to 4 minutes, stirring after 2½ minutes. Stir until smooth.

3. Place chocolate chips or squares in a small, heatproof bowl in hot water or top of a double boiler over hot (not boiling) water until melted.

If there is a tiny amount of steam or a few drops of water in the chocolate when it is being melted, it will harden or "tighten". If chocolate hardens while being melted, it can be returned to a creamy consistency by stirring in about 1 teaspoon shortening for each ounce of chocolate being melted.

Chocolate equivalent quantities:
1 package (6 ounces) semisweet chocolate chips equals 1 cup.
1 square (1 ounce) unsweetened chocolate equals 1 envelope premelted chocolate.
1 package (8 ounces) unsweetened chocolate equals 8 squares (1 ounce each).

In emergencies, 3 tablespoons unsweetened cocoa plus 1 tablespoon vegetable shortening can be substituted for 1 ounce unsweetened chocolate in some recipes.

Easter Bunny Cake

*Small Chocolate Cake
(below)
White Mountain
Frosting (page 16)
1 cup shredded coconut*

*Jelly beans or small
gumdrops
1 cup shredded coconut
Green food color
Construction paper*

Bake Small Chocolate Cake as directed. Cut cake into halves to make 2 semicircles; put halves together with White Mountain Frosting to form body. Place cake upright on cut edge on serving plate or tray.

Cut a notch about ⅓ of the way up one edge of body to form head as shown in diagram. Attach cut out piece for tail with wooden picks. Frost with remaining frosting, rounding body on sides. Sprinkle with 1 cup coconut. Cut ears from pink construction paper; press into top. Use jelly beans for eyes and nose.

Shake 1 cup shredded coconut and 2 or 3 drops green food color in tightly covered jar until evenly tinted. Surround bunny with tinted coconut. Add additional jelly beans if desired. 8 to 10 servings.

Small Chocolate Cake

*1 cup all-purpose flour
   or cake flour
1 cup sugar
¼ cup shortening
½ cup buttermilk
¼ cup water
½ teaspoon baking soda
½ teaspoon salt*

*¼ teaspoon baking
   powder
½ teaspoon vanilla
2 ounces melted
   unsweetened
   chocolate (cool)
1 egg*

Heat oven to 350°. Grease and flour round pan, 9 × 1½ inches. Beat all ingredients in large bowl on medium speed, scraping bowl constantly, until blended, 30 seconds. Beat on high speed, scraping bowl occasionally, 3 minutes. Pour into pan.

Bake until wooden pick inserted in center comes out clean, 30 to 35 minutes. Cool 10 minutes; remove from pan. Cool completely.

○ *Time-saver Tip:* Substitute any 8- or 9-inch cake layer for the Small Chocolate Cake. Substitute 1 package (7.2 ounces) fluffy white frosting mix for the White Mountain Frosting. Prepare as directed on package.

Cutting and Assembling Easter Bunny Cake

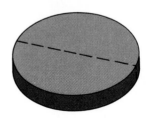

Cut cake into halves to make 2 semicircles.

Cut notch about ⅓ of the way up one edge of body to form head.

Attach cut out piece for tail with wooden pick.

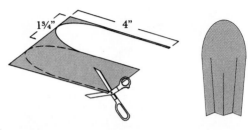

Cut 4 × 1¾ inch ears from pink construction paper. Fold as shown.

Easter Bunny Cake

Mother's Day Cake

Lady Baltimore Cake
  (below)
½ cup raisins, cut up
6 dried figs, cut up
3 tablespoons brandy
White Mountain
  Frosting (page 16)
½ cup chopped pecans
⅓ cup powdered sugar
5 drops red food color
6 square peppermint
  party mints

Bake Lady Baltimore Cake as directed. Mix raisins, figs and brandy; let stand until brandy is absorbed, about 1 hour. Prepare White Mountain Frosting; reserve ¼ cup for decorating. Stir raisin mixture and pecans into ⅔ cup of the remaining frosting. Fill layers with half of the filling; spread remaining filling over top of cake. Frost side and top of cake with remaining frosting.

Stir powdered sugar and food color into reserved frosting; place in decorating bag with writing tip #3. Write desired message on top of cake. Cut party mints diagonally into halves; arrange around top edge of cake. 10 to 14 servings.

Lady Baltimore Cake

2¼ cups all-purpose flour
1⅔ cups sugar
⅔ cup shortening
1¼ cups milk
3½ teaspoons baking
  powder
1 teaspoon salt
1 teaspoon vanilla
5 egg whites

Heat oven to 350°. Grease and flour 2 round pans, 8 × 1½ inches. Beat flour, sugar, shortening, milk, baking powder, salt and vanilla in large bowl on medium speed, scraping bowl constantly, until blended, about 30 seconds. Beat on high speed, scraping bowl occasionally, 2 minutes. Beat in egg whites on high speed, scraping bowl occasionally, 2 minutes. Pour into pans.

Bake until wooden pick inserted in center comes out clean, 30 to 35 minutes. Cool 10 minutes; remove from pans. Cool completely.

○ Time-saver Tip: Substitute 1 package (18.5 ounces) white cake mix with pudding for the Lady Baltimore Cake. Prepare and bake as directed on package. Substitute 1 package (7.2 ounces) fluffy white frosting mix for the White Mountain Frosting. Prepare as directed on package.

Father's Day Cake

Lord Baltimore Cake
  (below)
White Mountain
  Frosting (page 16)
½ cup sliced almonds
¼ cup toasted macaroon
  crumbs or ½ cup
  toasted flaked
  coconut
¼ cup finely chopped
  maraschino
  cherries, well
  drained
½ cup powdered sugar
2 teaspoons cocoa
1½ teaspoons water
3 or 4 maraschino
  cherries, cut into
  halves and well
  drained
Sliced almonds

Bake Lord Baltimore Cake as directed. Prepare White Mountain Frosting. Stir ½ cup almonds, the macaroon crumbs and ¼ cup cherries into ⅔ cup of the frosting. Fill layers with half of the almond mixture; spread remaining mixture over top. Frost top and side of cake with remaining frosting, making top smooth.

Mix powdered sugar, cocoa and water. If necessary, add water, a few drops at a time, until desired consistency. Place in decorating bag with writing tip #5; write desired message on top of cake. Arrange maraschino cherry halves and sliced almonds in design around top edge of cake. 12 to 16 servings.

Lord Baltimore Cake

2 cups all-purpose flour
1½ cups sugar
½ cup shortening (half
  margarine or butter,
  softened, if desired)
1 cup milk
3½ teaspoons baking
  powder
1 teaspoon salt
1 teaspoon vanilla
3 eggs

Heat oven to 350°. Grease and flour 2 round pans, 8 or 9 × 1½ inches. Beat all ingredients in large bowl on medium speed, scraping bowl constantly, until blended, about 30 seconds. Beat on high speed, scraping bowl occasionally, 3 minutes. Pour into pans.

Bake until wooden pick inserted in center comes out clean, 30 to 35 minutes. Cool 10 minutes; remove from pans. Cool completely.

○ Time-saver Tip: Substitute 1 package (18.5 ounces) yellow cake mix with pudding for the Lord Baltimore Cake. Prepare and bake as directed on package. Substitute 1 package (7.2 ounces) fluffy white frosting mix for the White Mountain Frosting. Prepare as directed on package.

Father's Day Cake, top, Mother's Day Cake, bottom

Flag Cake

Silver White Cake (below)
*Almond Butter Frosting
(below)*

*Blue and red paste food
color*

Bake Silver White Cake as directed. Reserve 4⅓ cups Almond Butter Frosting for decorating. Frost sides of cake with remaining frosting. Tint ⅓ cup of the reserved frosting with blue food color; spread in a rectangle on upper left corner of cake as base for stars.

Tint 1⅔ cups frosting with red food color; place in decorating bag with large open star tip #4B. Pipe stripes across top, bottom and center of cake; add 2 stripes at equal intervals above and below center stripe. Pipe white frosting between red stripes. Press out 50 white stars in alternate rows of 6 and 5 on blue rectangle with open star tip #18.

Silver White Cake

2¼ cups all-purpose flour
1⅔ cups sugar
⅔ cup shortening
1¼ cups milk
3½ teaspoons baking
    powder

1 teaspoon salt
1 teaspoon almond
    extract
5 egg whites

Heat oven to 350°. Grease and flour rectangular pan, 13×9×2 inches. Beat flour, sugar, shortening, milk, baking powder, salt and almond extract in large bowl on medium speed, scraping bowl constantly, until blended, about 30 seconds. Beat on high speed, scraping bowl occasionally, 2 minutes. Beat in egg whites on high speed, scraping bowl occasionaly, 2 minutes. Pour into pan.

Bake until wooden pick inserted in center comes out clean, 40 to 45 minutes. Cool 10 minutes; remove from pan. Cool completely.

Almond Butter Frosting

9 cups powdered
    sugar
1 cup margarine or
    butter, softened

1 tablespoon almond
    extract
½ cup milk

Beat all ingredients on medium speed until smooth and spreading consistency. If necessary, stir in additional milk, 1 teaspoon at a time.

Drum Cake (page 36), top, Flag Cake, bottom

Drum Cake

Chocolate Buttermilk
  Cake (below)
Vanilla Butter Frosting
  (below)
Red or green food color,
  if desired

12 to 16 candy sticks,
  peppermint sticks or
  licorice rope twists
2 lollipops

Bake Chocolate Buttermilk Cake as directed. Tint half of the Vanilla Butter Frosting (about 1¼ cups) with food color; reserve. Fill layers with ⅓ cup of the remaining frosting. Frost side of cake with tinted frosting. Frost top of cake with remaining frosting. Make circular design on top with decorating comb if desired.

Press candy sticks at angles into frosting around side of cake. Press licorice into frosting around top and bottom of cake for border of drum. Place lollipops on top for drumsticks. 12 to 16 servings.

Chocolate Buttermilk Cake

2¼ cups all-purpose flour
1¾ cups sugar
½ cup shortening
1½ cups buttermilk
1½ teaspoons baking soda
1 teaspoon salt

1 teaspoon vanilla
2 ounces melted
  unsweetened
  chocolate (cool)
2 eggs
½ cup chopped nuts

Heat oven to 350°. Grease and flour 2 round pans, 8 × 1½ inches. Beat all ingredients in large bowl on medium speed, scraping bowl constantly, until blended, 30 seconds. Beat on high speed, scraping bowl occasionally, 2 minutes. Pour into pans.

Bake until wooden pick inserted in center comes out clean, 35 to 40 minutes. Cool 10 minutes; remove from pans. Cool completely.

Vanilla Butter Frosting

3 cups powdered sugar
⅓ cup margarine or
  butter, softened

1½ teaspoons vanilla
2 tablespoons milk

Beat all ingredients on medium speed until smooth and spreading consistency. If necessary, stir in additional milk, ½ teaspoon at a time.

○ Time-saver Tip: Substitute 1 package (18.5 ounces) devils food cake mix with pudding for the Chocolate Buttermilk Cake. Prepare and bake as directed on package. Substitute 1 package (14.3 ounces) creamy white frosting mix for the Vanilla Butter Frosting. Prepare as directed on package.

Cat Cake

Peanut Cake (below)
Creamy Cocoa Frosting
  (below)

Large yellow gumdrop
Small black gumdrop
Black shoestring licorice

Bake Peanut Cake as directed. Cut 1 layer as shown in diagram. Freeze cut pieces uncovered about 1 hour for easier frosting if desired. Arrange uncut layer and the pieces as shown in diagram to form cat on large tray or aluminum foil-covered cardboard, about 18 × 12 inches.

Join all parts and frost sides and top of cake with Creamy Cocoa Frosting. Use yellow gumdrop slices for eyes, black gumdrop for nose and shoestring licorice for whiskers and lines on eyes and front paws. 12 to 16 servings.

Peanut Cake

2 cups all-purpose flour
1½ cups sugar
½ cup shortening (half
  margarine or butter,
  softened, if desired)
1 cup milk

3½ teaspoons baking
  powder
1 teaspoon salt
1 teaspoon vanilla
3 eggs
½ cup finely chopped
  peanuts

Heat oven to 350°. Grease and flour 2 round pans, 8 or 9 × 1½ inches. Beat all ingredients in large bowl on medium speed, scraping bowl constantly, until blended, about 30 seconds. Beat on high speed, scraping bowl occasionally, 3 minutes. Pour into pans.

Bake until wooden pick inserted in center comes out clean, 30 to 35 minutes. Cool 10 minutes; remove from pans. Cool completely.

Creamy Cocoa Frosting

3 cups powdered sugar
½ cup cocoa
½ cup margarine or
  butter, softened

1 teaspoon vanilla
3 tablespoons water

Beat all ingredients on medium speed until smooth and spreading consistency. If necessary, stir in additional water, ½ teaspoon at a time.

○ Time-saver Tip: Substitute 1 package (18.5 ounces) yellow cake mix with pudding for the Peanut Cake. Prepare and bake as directed on package except stir ½ cup finely chopped peanuts into batter.

Cat Cake

Cutting and Assembling Cat Cake

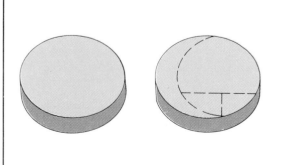

Cut 1 layer to form head, ears and tail of cat.

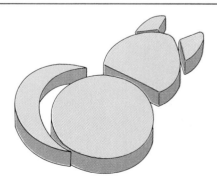

Arrange uncut layer and pieces to form cat.

Halloween Cupcakes

Chocolate Cupcakes (below)

Creamy Orange Frosting (below)
Gumdrop Cats (below)

Bake Chocolate Cupcakes as directed. Frost cupcakes with Creamy Orange Frosting. Decorate tops with Gumdrop Cats. 2 dozen cupcakes.

Chocolate Cupcakes

1²/₃ cups all-purpose flour	1 teaspoon baking soda
1½ cups sugar	½ teaspoon baking
½ cup cocoa	powder
½ cup shortening	½ teaspoon salt
1 cup hot water	2 eggs

Heat oven to 350°. Beat all ingredients in large bowl on medium speed, scraping bowl constantly, until blended, about 30 seconds. Beat on high speed, scraping bowl occasionally, 3 minutes. Pour into paper-lined medium muffin cups, 2½ × 1¼ inches, filling each ⅔ full.

Bake until wooden pick inserted in center comes out clean, 20 to 25 minutes. Immediately remove from pan; cool completely.

Creamy Orange Frosting

2½ cups powdered sugar	3 tablespoons orange
2 tablespoons shortening	juice
1 tablespoon margarine	1 tablespoon lemon
or butter, softened	juice
1 teaspoon finely	Red and yellow food
shredded orange peel	color
¼ teaspoon salt	

Beat all ingredients except food color on medium speed until frosting is smooth and spreading consistency. Stir in 1 or 2 drops each food color.

Gumdrop Cats

Cut a large black gumdrop into 3 pieces as shown in diagram. Use small rounded top piece for head and largest piece for body. Cut tail and ears from third piece.

○ *Time-saver Tip:* Substitute 1 package (18.5 ounces) chocolate fudge cake mix with pudding for the Chocolate Cupcakes. Prepare and bake as directed on package for cupcakes. Substitute 1 tub (16.5 ounces) orange ready-to-spread frosting for the Creamy Orange Frosting.

Halloween Cupcakes

Gumdrop Cat Preparation

Cut gumdrop into 3 pieces. Use rounded top piece for head, largest piece for body, third piece for tail and ears.

Cranberry Jewel Cake

Silver White Cake (below)   Frosted Cranberries
Cranberry Filling (below)   (right)
Creamy Frosting (below)   Mint leaves

Bake Silver White Cake as directed. Fill layers with 1 cup Cranberry Filling. Frost side of cake with Creamy Frosting, forming ¼-inch ridge above top of cake. Spread top of cake with remaining filling. Decorate with Frosted Cranberries and mint leaves. 10 to 14 servings.

Silver White Cake

2¼ cups all-purpose flour   3½ teaspoons baking
1⅔ cups sugar   powder
 ⅔ cup shortening   1 teaspoon salt
1¼ cups milk   1 teaspoon vanilla
                               5 egg whites

Heat oven to 350°. Grease and flour 2 round pans, 8 or 9×1½ inches. Beat flour, sugar, shortening, milk, baking powder, salt, and vanilla in large bowl on medium speed, scraping bowl constantly, until blended, about 30 seconds. Beat on high speed, scraping bowl occasionally, 2 minutes. Beat in egg whites on high speed, scraping bowl occasionally, 2 minutes. Pour into pans.

Bake until wooden pick inserted in center comes out clean, 30 to 35 minutes. Cool 10 minutes; remove from pans. Cool completely.

Cranberry Filling

1 can (8¼ ounces)   3 tablespoons cornstarch
   crushed pineapple,   1 can (16 ounces)
   drained (reserve ¼   whole cranberry sauce
   cup syrup)   ¼ teaspoon red food color

Mix reserved syrup and cornstarch in saucepan. Stir in remaining ingredients. Cook, stirring constantly, until mixture thickens and boils. Boil and stir 1 minute. Refrigerate until cool.

Creamy Frosting

2¼ cups powdered sugar   1 teaspoon vanilla
 ¼ cup margarine or   1 tablespoon milk
   butter

Beat all ingredients on medium speed until smooth and spreading consistency. If necessary, stir in additional milk, ½ teaspoon at a time.

Frosted Cranberries

Dip cranberries into water, then dip into granulated sugar. Dry cranberries on wire racks before adding to cake.

○ *Time-saver Tip:* Substitute 1 package (18.5 ounces) white cake mix with pudding for the Silver White Cake. Prepare and bake as directed on package. Substitute 1 tub (16.5 ounces) vanilla ready-to-spread frosting or 1 package (14.3 ounces) creamy white frosting mix for the Creamy Frosting. Prepare frosting mix as directed on package.

Cranberry Jewel Cake

Thanksgiving Cake

Mocha Spice Cake
(below)
Caramel Fluffy
Frosting (below)
1 tablespoon cocoa

2 tablespoons powdered
sugar
1/4 teaspoon water
Clusters of grapes

Bake Mocha Spice Cake as directed. Reserve 1½ cups of the Caramel Fluffy Frosting for decorating. Fill and frost layers with remaining frosting, making top smooth. Sift cocoa over ¾ cup of the reserved frosting; fold in until blended. Reserve 2 tablespoons cocoa frosting for writing message.

Place remaining cocoa frosting in decorating bag with closed star tip #30. Pipe cornucopia onto top of cake by starting at narrow end and increasing pressure and width of lines.

Stir powdered sugar and water into reserved cocoa frosting. If necessary, stir in additional water, a few drops at a time. Place in decorating bag with writing tip #2; write desired message on cake. Pipe shell border around base and top edge of cake with remaining reserved frosting and open star tip #18 (see page 9). Arrange grapes at opening of cornucopia. 12 to 16 servings.

Mocha Spice Cake

2 cups all-purpose flour
1½ cups sugar
½ cup shortening (half
margarine or butter,
softened, if desired)
1 cup milk
2 tablespoons cocoa
3½ teaspoons baking
powder
1½ teaspoons instant
coffee

1 teaspoon ground
cinnamon
1 teaspoon ground
nutmeg
½ teaspoon ground
cloves
½ teaspoon salt
½ teaspoon vanilla
3 eggs

Heat oven to 350°. Grease and flour 2 round pans, 9 × 1½ inches. Beat all ingredients in large bowl on medium speed, scraping bowl constantly, until blended, 30 seconds. Beat on high speed, scraping bowl occasionally, 3 minutes. Pour into pans.

Bake until wooden pick inserted in center comes out clean, 30 to 35 minutes. Cool 10 minutes; remove from pans. Cool completely.

Caramel Fluffy Frosting

¾ cup packed brown
sugar
1/3 cup light corn syrup

3 tablespoons water
3 egg whites
½ teaspoon vanilla

Mix brown sugar, corn syrup and water in 1-quart saucepan. Cover and heat to rolling boil over medium heat. Uncover and boil rapidly until candy thermometer registers 242° or until small amount of mixture dropped into very cold water forms a firm ball that holds its shape until pressed.

As mixture boils, beat egg whites in small bowl just until stiff peaks form. Pour hot syrup very slowly in a thin stream into egg whites, beating constantly on medium speed. Add vanilla; beat on high speed until stiff peaks form.

○ *Time-saver Tip:* Substitute 1 package (18.5 ounces) yellow cake mix with pudding for the Mocha Spice Cake. Prepare and bake as directed on package except add 2 tablespoons cocoa, 1½ teaspoons instant coffee, 1 teaspoon ground cinnamon, 1 teaspoon ground nutmeg and ½ teaspoon ground cloves before beating.

BEATING TIPS

Our cakes have been tested with both the portable and standard electric mixer since surveys show that the majority of mixers in use in the United States are the portable type. Standard mixers are usually more powerful than portables so, for the initial step of beating layer cake ingredients until blended, reduce the speed of the standard mixer to low to prevent splattering.

You can also mix by hand. Stir the ingredients to moisten and blend them; then beat 150 strokes for every minute of beating time (3 minutes equals 450 strokes). You'll need practice before this seems easy; while you're practicing, cake volume may decrease.

Thanksgiving Cake, Top, Snowman Cake (page 42), bottom

Snowman Cake

Double Chocolate Cake (below)
White Mountain Frosting (page 16)
1 cup flaked coconut
4 or 5 semisweet chocolate chips
2 large green gumdrops
2 large black gumdrops
Red shoestring licorice
2 chocolate-covered marshmallow cookies

Bake Double Chocolate Cake as directed. Arrange 8-inch layer for head of snowman and 9-inch layer for body on large tray or aluminum foil-covered cardboard, about 18 × 10 inches. Frost layers with White Mountain Frosting, joining them together.

Sprinkle with flaked coconut. Use chocolate chips for buttons, green gumdrops for eyes, black gum-drops for eyebrows and nose and red shoestring licorice for mouth and muffler. Place chocolate-covered cookie on each side of head for earmuffs. 12 to 16 servings.

Double Chocolate Cake

2¼ cups all-purpose flour
1¾ cups sugar
½ cup shortening
1½ cups buttermilk
1½ teaspoons baking soda
1 teaspoon salt
1 teaspoon vanilla
2 ounces melted unsweetened chocolate (cool)
2 eggs
1 cup miniature chocolate chips

Heat oven to 350°. Grease and flour round pan, 8 × 1½ inches, and round pan, 9 × 1½ inches. Beat all ingredients except chocolate chips in large bowl on medium speed, scraping bowl constantly, until blended, about 30 seconds. Beat on high speed, scraping bowl occasionally, 2 minutes. Fold in chocolate chips. Pour into pans. (Batter in pans should be the same level — measure depth of bat-ter with a wooden pick.)

Bake until wooden pick inserted in center comes out clean and cake starts to pull away from side of pan, 35 to 40 minutes. Cool 10 minutes; remove from pans. Cool completely.

○ Time-saver Tip: Substitute 1 package (18.5 ounces) devils food cake mix with pudding for the Double Chocolate Cake. Prepare and bake as directed on package except decrease water to 1 cup and stir 1 cup miniature chocolate chips into batter. Substitute 1 package (7.2 ounces) fluffy white frost-ing mix for the White Mountain Frosting. Prepare as directed on package.

Spring Flower Cake

Yellow Layer Cake (below)
Lemon Butter Frosting (below)
Red, yellow and green food color

Bake Yellow Layer Cake as directed. Split cake to make 4 layers (see page 12). Reserve ½ cup Lemon Butter Frosting for decorating. Fill layers with about ⅓ cup frosting each, alternating pink and orange layers. Frost cake.

Tint 3 tablespoons reserved frosting pink with 1 drop red food color, tint 3 tablespoons frosting orange with 2 drops yellow and 1 drop red food color and tint remaining 2 tablespoons frosting green with 1 drop green food color. Make 6 to 8 rosettes with star tip #32 (see page 8) and pink frosting on top edge of cake; make rosettes with orange frosting between each pink flower. Make leaves with green frosting (see page 9). 12 to 16 servings.

Yellow Layer Cake

2 cups all-purpose flour
1½ cups sugar
½ cup shortening (half margarine or butter, softened, if desired)
1 cup milk
3½ teaspoons baking powder
1 teaspoon salt
1 teaspoon vanilla
3 eggs
Red and yellow food color

Heat oven to 350°. Grease and flour 2 round pans, 8 or 9 × 1½ inches. Beat all ingredients except food color in large bowl on medium speed, scraping bowl constantly, until blended, about 30 seconds. Beat on high speed, scraping bowl occasionally, 3 minutes. Tint half of the batter pink with 6 drops red food color. Tint remaining batter orange with 4 drops yellow and 2 drops red food color. Pour batters into separate pans.

Bake until wooden pick inserted in center comes out clean, 30 to 35 minutes. Cool 10 minutes; re-move from pans. Cool completely.

Lemon Butter Frosting

6 cups powdered sugar
⅔ cup margarine or butter, softened
¼ cup lemon juice

Beat all ingredients on high speed until frosting is smooth and spreading consistency. If necessary, stir in additional lemon juice, 1 teaspoon at a time.

Spring Flower Cake, top, Nosegay Cupcakes (page 44), bottom

Nosegay Cupcakes

*Silver White Cupcakes
(below)*

*Lemon Frosting (below)
Decorator Frosting (right)*

Bake Silver White Cupcakes as directed. Frost with Lemon Frosting. Place violet Decorator Frosting in decorating bag with special petal tip #101. Hold tip with wide end at center. Bring tip out and back to center to form a narrow petal about ½ inch long as shown. Pipe 2 more petals ¼ inch long. Add 2 petals ½ inch long. Place yellow frosting in decorating bag with writing tip #3. Place 2 dots in center of each violet. 2½ dozen cupcakes.

Silver White Cupcakes

2¼ cups all-purpose flour	1 teaspoon salt
1⅔ cups sugar	1 teaspoon lemon
⅔ cup shortening	extract
1¼ cups milk	5 egg whites
3½ teaspoons baking powder	

Heat oven to 350°. Beat flour, sugar, shortening, milk, baking powder, salt and lemon extract in large bowl on medium speed, scraping bowl constantly, until blended, about 30 seconds. Beat on high speed, scraping bowl occasionally, 2 minutes. Beat in egg whites on high speed, scraping bowl occasionally, 2 minutes. Pour into paper-lined medium muffin cups, 2½ × 1¼ inches, filling each ½ full.

Bake until wooden pick inserted in center comes out clean, 20 to 25 minutes. Immediately remove from pan; cool completely.

Lemon Frosting

3½ cups powdered sugar	2 tablespoons lemon
⅔ cup all-purpose flour	juice
½ cup margarine or butter, softened	2 tablespoons water
¼ teaspoon salt	1 tablespoon light corn syrup
1 teaspoon finely shredded lemon peel	3 drops yellow food color

Beat all ingredients on medium speed until smooth and spreading consistency. If necessary, stir in additional water, 1 teaspoon at a time.

Decorator Frosting

2 cups powdered sugar	1 tablespoon milk
½ cup shortening	1 drop yellow food color
½ teaspoon almond extract	1/16 teaspoon violet paste food color

Beat all ingredients except food colors on medium speed until frosting is smooth and desired consistency. If necessary, stir in additional milk, ½ teaspoon at a time. Tint ¼ cup of the frosting with yellow food color for centers of violets. Tint remaining frosting violet with paste food color.

○ *Time-saver Tip:* Substitute 1 package (18.5 ounces) white cake mix with pudding for the Silver White Cupcakes. Prepare and bake as directed on package for cupcakes. Substitute 1 package (14.3 ounces) lemon frosting mix for the Lemon Frosting. Prepare as directed on package.

Piping Violet

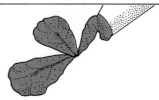

Hold tip with wide end at center. Bring tip out and back to center to form a narrow petal about ½ inch long. Pipe 2 more petals ¼ inch long. Add 2 petals ½ inch long.

Using yellow frosting, place 2 dots in center of violet.

Pastel Swirl Cupcakes

Silver White Cupcakes   *Buttercream Frosting*
  (below)   *(below)*

Bake Silver White Cupcakes as directed. Place Buttercream Frosting in decorating bag with large open star tip #4B. Pipe in a spiral cone shape onto cupcakes. 2½ dozen cupcakes.

Silver White Cupcakes

2¼ cups all-purpose flour   3½ teaspoons baking
1⅔ cups sugar   powder
⅔ cup shortening   1 teaspoon salt
1¼ cups milk   1 teaspoon vanilla
                          5 egg whites

Heat oven to 350°. Beat flour, sugar, shortening, milk, baking powder, salt and vanilla in large bowl on medium speed, scraping bowl constantly, until blended, about 30 seconds. Beat on high speed, scraping bowl occasionally, 2 minutes. Beat in egg whites on high speed, scraping bowl occasionally, 2 minutes. Pour into paper-lined medium muffin cups, 2½ × 1¼ inches, filling each ½ full.

Bake until wooden pick inserted in center comes out clean, 20 to 25 minutes. Immediately remove from pan; cool completely.

Buttercream Frosting

8 cups powdered sugar   2 teaspoons almond
1 cup margarine or   extract
   butter, softened   ⅓ cup milk
1 cup shortening   Assorted food color

Beat all ingredients except food color on medium speed until frosting is smooth and desired consistency. If necessary, stir in additional milk, 1 teaspoon at a time. Tint portions of frosting pastel colors with desired food color.

○ *Time-saver Tip:* Substitute 1 package (18.5 ounces) white cake mix with pudding for the Silver White Cupcakes. Prepare and bake as directed on package for cupcakes.

Pastel Swirl Cupcakes

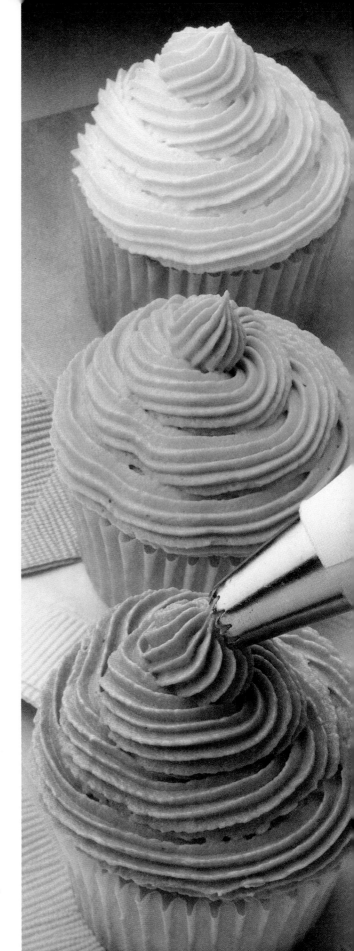

Summer Fruit Cake

Butterscotch Cake (below)	2 nectarines or peaches, sliced
½ cup apple jelly	2 kiwis, peeled and sliced
Spiced Whipped Cream (below)	½ cup blueberries
	½ cup strawberries, cut into halves

Bake Butterscotch Cake as directed. Heat apple jelly until melted; brush half of the jelly on layers before assembling. Spread 1 layer with ½ cup of the Spiced Whipped Cream; arrange half of the nectarine slices on top. Top with remaining layer. Place remaining Spiced Whipped Cream in decorating bag with open star tip #199; pipe vertical rows up and down side of cake.

Arrange fruit in attractive design on cake; brush with remaining jelly. Refrigerate any remaining cake. 12 to 14 servings.

Butterscotch Cake

2¼ cups all-purpose flour	3 teaspoons baking powder
1¾ cups packed brown sugar	1 teaspoon salt
½ cup shortening	1 teaspoon vanilla
1 cup milk	2 eggs

Heat oven to 350°. Grease and flour 2 round pans, 9 × 1½ inches. Beat all ingredients in large bowl on medium speed, scraping bowl constantly, until blended, 30 seconds. Beat on high speed, scraping bowl occasionally, 3 minutes. Pour into pans.

Bake until wooden pick inserted in center comes out clean, 30 to 35 minutes. Cool 10 minutes; remove from pans. Cool completely.

Spiced Whipped Cream

| 2 cups chilled whipping cream | ½ teaspoon ground cinnamon |
| ¼ cup sugar | ¼ teaspoon ground mace |

Beat all ingredients in chilled bowl until stiff.

○ *Time-saver Tip:* Substitute 1 package (18.5 ounces) yellow cake mix with pudding for the Butterscotch Cake. Prepare and bake as directed on package.

Summer Fruit Cake

Garden Cake

Garden Cake

Zucchini Cake (below)　　*Green, yellow and red food*
Cream Cheese Frosting　　*color*
(below)

Bake Zucchini Cake as directed. Prepare Cream Cheese Frosting. Reserve 1 cup frosting for decorating. Frost cake with remaining frosting.

Tint ⅔ cup of the reserved frosting green with 3 drops green food color. Tint ⅓ cup of the reserved frosting yellow with 1 drop yellow food color; reserve 2 tablespoons yellow frosting. Tint remaining yellow frosting orange with 2 drops red food color. (Keep all frostings covered to prevent drying.)

Place green frosting in decorating bag with writing tip #2. Pipe straight lines on cake to divide into 15

servings. Place orange frosting in decorating bag with petal tip #103; pipe tulips onto 6 of the servings. Place yellow frosting in decorating bag with drop flower tip #217 (see page 8). Pipe drop flowers onto 3 servings.

Pipe parsley, stems for tulips and leaves for zucchini with green frosting and writing tip #2. Form zucchini with large writing tip #7, starting at leaf end and increasing pressure slightly. Pipe leaves for tulips and drop flowers with green frosting and leaf tip #352. Pipe border with star tip #18. 15 servings.

Zucchini Cake

⅓ cup boiling water	1 teaspoon ground
2 cups finely chopped	cinnamon
zucchini (about 3	1 teaspoon ground cloves
medium)	1 teaspoon ground
2 cups all-purpose flour	nutmeg
1¼ cups sugar	1 teaspoon vanilla
½ cup vegetable oil	3 eggs
1¼ teaspoons baking soda	1 cup chopped nuts
1 teaspoon salt	

Pour boiling water over zucchini in large bowl. Grease and flour rectangular pan, 13 × 9 × 2 inches.

Heat oven to 350°. Beat zucchini mixture and remaining ingredients on medium speed, scraping bowl constantly, until blended, about 1 minute. Beat on medium speed, scraping bowl occasionally, 2 minutes. Pour into pan.

Bake until wooden pick inserted in center comes out clean, 45 to 50 minutes. Cool 10 minutes; remove from pan if desired. Cool completely.

Cream Cheese Frosting

6 cups powdered sugar	1 package (3 ounces)
¾ cup margarine or	cream cheese, softened
butter, softened	¼ cup lemon juice

Beat all ingredients on medium speed until smooth and spreading consistency. If necessary, stir in additional lemon juice, 1 teaspoon at a time.

Autumn Festival Cake

Spiced Angel Food
Cake (below)
1½ cups chilled
whipping cream
⅓ cup powdered sugar
2 to 4 tablespoons dark
crème de cacao
Frosted Grapes (below)

Bake Spiced Angel Food Cake as directed. Beat whipping cream and ⅓ cup powdered sugar in chilled bowl until stiff; fold in crème de cacao. Frost cake; refrigerate. Just before serving, decorate cake with Frosted Grapes. Refrigerate any remaining cake. 12 to 16 servings.

Spiced Angel Food Cake

1½ cups powdered
sugar
1 cup cake flour
1½ cups egg whites
(about 12)
1½ teaspoons cream of
tartar
1 cup granulated
sugar
1 teaspoon pumpkin
pie spice
¼ teaspoon salt

Heat oven to 375°. Mix powdered sugar and flour. Beat egg whites and cream of tartar in large bowl on medium speed until foamy. Beat in granulated sugar on high speed, 2 tablespoons at a time; continue beating until stiff and glossy. Add pumpkin pie spice and salt with the last addition of sugar. Do not underbeat.

Sprinkle flour-sugar mixture, about ¼ cup at a time, over meringue, folding in just until flour-sugar mixture disappears. Push batter into ungreased tube pan, 10 × 4 inches. Cut gently through batter with metal spatula.

Bake until cracks feel dry and top springs back when touched lightly, 30 to 35 minutes. Invert pan on heatproof funnel; let hang until cake is cold. Remove from pan.

Frosted Grapes

Dip small clusters of Tokay grapes into water, then dip into granulated sugar. Dry clusters on wire racks before adding to cake.

○ *Time-saver Tip:* Substitute 1 package (16 ounces) white angel food cake mix for the Spiced Angel Food Cake. Prepare and bake as directed on the package.

Autumn Festival Cake

Chrysanthemum Cake

Cutting Chrysanthemum

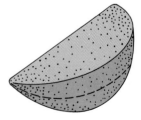

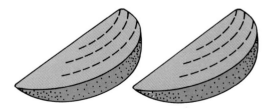

With knife or scissors, cut candy slice lengthwise into 2 thin slices; dip into sugar.

With curved rim as guide, cut each slice into 4 curved petals, leaving them attached at one end.

Chrysanthemum Cake

Burnt Sugar Cake
  (below)
Mincemeat-Orange
  Filling (right)

Satiny Beige Frosting
  (right)
10 to 12 candy orange
  slices (about ⅓
  pound)

Prepare Burnt Sugar Cake as directed. Fill layers with Mincemeat-Orange Filling. Frost cake with Satiny Beige Frosting.

With knife or scissors, cut each of 8 candy slices lengthwise into 2 thin slices as shown in diagram; dip into sugar. With curved rim as guide, cut each thin slice into 4 slender curved petals, leaving them attached at one end; dip into sugar after each cut.

To form flower, place each group of 4 petals on frosted cake with tips outward toward edge of circle, curving upward. Cut separate petals to fill in; bend some into loops for center. 14 to 16 servings.

Burnt Sugar Cake

1½ cups sugar
½ cup boiling water
2 eggs, separated
½ cup margarine or
  butter, softened
1 teaspoon vanilla

2¼ cups all-purpose
  flour
3 teaspoons baking
  powder
1 teaspoon salt
1 cup milk

Heat ½ cup of the sugar in heavy 8-inch skillet over medium heat, stirring constantly, until sugar is melted and golden brown. Remove from heat; stir in boiling water slowly. Cook over low heat, stirring constantly, until sugar lumps are dissolved. Add enough water to syrup, if necessary, to measure ½ cup; cool.

Heat oven to 375°. Grease and flour 2 square pans, 8×8×2 inches or 2 round pans, 9×1½ inches. Beat egg whites in small bowl until foamy. Beat in ½ cup of the sugar, about 1 tablespoon at a time; continue beating until very stiff and glossy. Reserve meringue.

Beat remaining sugar, the egg yolks, margarine and vanilla in large bowl on medium speed, scraping bowl constantly, until blended, 30 seconds. Beat on high speed, scraping bowl occasionally, 5 minutes. Beat in syrup. Beat in flour, baking powder and salt alternately with milk on low speed. Fold into reserved meringue. Pour into pans.

Bake until wooden pick inserted in center comes out clean, 25 to 30 minutes. Cool 10 minutes; remove from pans. Cool completely.

Mincemeat-Orange Filling

1 tablespoon packed
  brown sugar
1 tablespoon cornstarch
⅓ cup orange juice

½ cup mincemeat*
1 teaspoon finely
  shredded orange peel,
  if desired

Mix brown sugar and cornstarch. Gradually stir in orange juice and mincemeat. Cook and stir over medium heat until thickened. Stir in orange peel.

*⅓ cup raisins can be substituted for the mincemeat. If necessary, stir in additional orange juice, 1 teaspoon at a time.

Satiny Beige Frosting

½ cup packed brown
  sugar
¼ cup light corn syrup

2 tablespoons water
2 egg whites
½ teaspoon vanilla

Mix brown sugar, corn syrup and water in 1-quart saucepan. Cover and heat to rolling boil over medium heat. Uncover and boil rapidly until candy thermometer registers 242° or until small amount of mixture dropped into very cold water forms a firm ball that holds its shape until pressed.

As mixture boils, beat egg whites in small bowl just until stiff peaks form. Pour hot syrup very slowly in a thin stream into egg whites, beating constantly on medium speed. Add vanilla; beat on high speed until stiff peaks form.

○ Time-saver Tip: Substitute 1 package (18.5 ounces) yellow cake mix with pudding for the Burnt Sugar Cake. Prepare and bake as directed on package. Substitute 1 package (7.2 ounces) fluffy white frosting mix for the Satiny Beige Frosting. Prepare as directed on package.

Celebration Cakes

Classic White Wedding Cake

For the entire wedding cake prepare 6 recipes Silver White Cake, 2 recipes Creamy White Frosting and as many recipes White Decorator Frosting as necessary. Prepare batter just before baking; measure ingredients ahead if desired. Bake cake layers the day before they are to be assembled or bake them earlier and freeze.

Silver White Cake (right)   White Decorator Frosting
Creamy White Frosting   (right)
   (right)

Grease and flour 1 round pan, 10 × 2 inches. Prepare 1 recipe Silver White Cake. Pour 4½ cups batter into pan. Bake until top springs back when touched lightly in center, 45 to 50 minutes. Cool 15 minutes; remove from pan. Cool completely.

Grease and flour 1 round pan, 14 × 2 inches, and 1 round pan, 6 × 2 inches. Prepare 2 recipes Silver White Cake, 1 recipe at a time. Pour 1½ cups batter into 6-inch pan; pour 7¾ cups batter into 14-inch pan. Bake until top springs back when touched lightly in center, 6-inch layer 35 to 40 minutes, 14-inch layer 50 to 55 minutes. Cool 15 minutes; remove from pans. Cool completely.

Repeat above process, making a total of 6 layers. Each tier of wedding cake will consist of 2 layers. (Height must measure 3 inches total or 1½ inches per layer.) Tops of layers should be flat for ease in stacking. Slice off rounded tops if necessary.

Prepare 1 recipe Creamy White Frosting. Place 14-inch layer on tray or mirror. Fill and frost 14-inch tier, using 1 cup frosting to fill and remaining to frost. Place aluminum foil-covered 10-inch cardboard circle on first tier. Place 10-inch layer on cardboard.

Prepare 1 recipe Creamy White Frosting. Fill and frost 10-inch tier, using ¾ cup frosting to fill and 2 cups to frost. Place aluminum foil-covered 6-inch cardboard circle on second tier. Place 6-inch layer on cardboard. Fill and frost 6-inch tier, using ⅓ cup frosting to fill and remaining to frost.

Prepare White Decorator Frosting, one recipe at a time. Place in decorating bag with petal tip #103. Make desired number of roses (see page 10); refrigerate until ready to use. Pipe shell border around top edge and base of each tier with open star tip #18. Arrange roses on cake as desired. Pipe leaves onto roses with leaf tip #352. 70 servings, 2 × 1½ inches.

Silver White Cake

2¼ cups all-purpose flour   1 teaspoon salt
1⅔ cups sugar   1 teaspoon almond
 ⅔ cup shortening   extract or vanilla
1¼ cups milk   5 egg whites
3½ teaspoons baking
   powder

Heat oven to 325°. Beat flour, sugar, shortening, milk, baking powder, salt and almond extract in large bowl on medium speed, scraping bowl constantly, until blended, 30 seconds. Beat on high speed, scraping bowl occasionally, 2 minutes. Beat in egg whites on high speed, scraping bowl occasionally, 2 minutes. Bake and cool layers as directed.

Creamy White Frosting

6 cups powdered sugar   ½ cup plus 2 tablespoons
¾ cup shortening   milk
¾ teaspoon almond
   extract

Beat all ingredients on medium speed until smooth and spreading consistency. If necessary, stir in additional milk, 1 teaspoon at a time.

White Decorator Frosting

Prepare Creamy White Frosting as directed except increase powdered sugar to 6¼ cups and decrease milk to ½ cup. Decorate cake as directed.

Layers of other sizes can be made; see directions below. One recipe Silver White Cake yields about 5 cups batter.

Pan Size	Amount of Batter	Baking Time
7 × 2-inch round	2 cups	40 to 45 minutes
9 × 2-inch round	3 cups	40 to 45 minutes
10 × 2-inch round	4½ cups	45 to 50 minutes
12 × 2-inch round	5 cups	45 to 50 minutes

Pictured on preceding page: Classic White Wedding Cake (above)

How to Cut a Wedding Cake

Use a thin, sharp or serrated knife. Insert knife into cake, keeping point down and handle up. Slice, pulling knife toward you. If frosting sticks, dip knife in hot water or wipe with damp paper towel after cutting each slice.

Round Tiered Cake

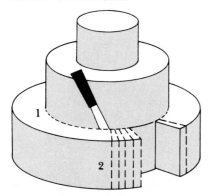 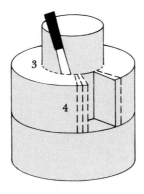 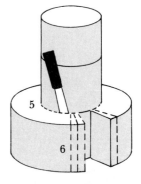

Cut vertically through bottom layer at edge of second layer as indicated by dotted line 1; then cut into wedges as indicated by dotted line 2.

Follow same procedure with middle layer by cutting vertically through second layer at edge of top layer as indicated by dotted line 3; then cut into wedges as indicated by dotted line 4.

Return to bottom layer and cut along dotted line 5; cut into wedges as indicated by dotted line 6. Separate remaining layers (traditionally the top layer is frozen for the couple's first anniversary); cut into desired sizes.

Square Tiered Cake

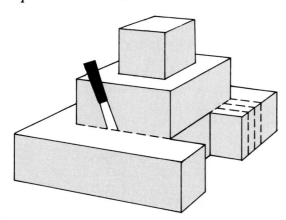

The cutting procedure for a square tiered cake is essentially the same as for a round tiered cake. Cut bottom layer all around; then cut middle layer. Return to bottom layer and continue as directed above.

Servings Per 2-Layer Tier

Each serving measures 2 × 1 inch from a tier 3 inches high.

Layer	Round	Square
6-inch	10	18
7-inch	15	—
8-inch	22	32
9-inch	28	40
10-inch	35	50
12-inch	50	72
14-inch	70	98
16-inch	100	128
18 × 12-inch rectangular	108	

Marble Wedding Cake

Assembling Marble Wedding Cake

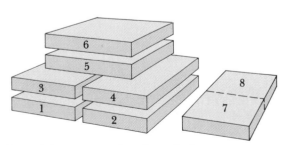

Place 2 layers together lengthwise on tray; spread with frosting. Place 2 layers directly on top; frost sides and top. Place fifth layer on first tier; frost top. Place sixth layer on fifth; frost sides and top.

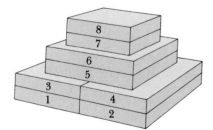

Cut seventh layer into halves. Place half on second tier; frost top. Place remaining half on top; frost sides and top.

Marble Wedding Cake

For the entire wedding cake prepare 7 recipes Marble Cake, 4 recipes Coffee Cream Frosting, 2 recipes Chocolate Decorator Frosting and 1 recipe Chocolate Leaves. Prepare batter just before baking; measure ingredients ahead if desired. Bake cake layers the day before they are to be assembled or bake them earlier and freeze.

Marble Cake (below)	Chocolate Decorator
Coffee Cream Frosting	Frosting (right)
(right)	Chocolate Leaves (right)

Bake Marble Cake as directed. Repeat 6 times. Prepare Coffee Cream Frosting, repeating as necessary. Place 2 layers upside down and together lengthwise on large tray or mirror, about 20 × 15 inches. Spread with frosting. Place 2 more layers directly on top of frosted layers as shown in diagram. Frost sides and top.

Place aluminum foil-covered cardboard rectangle, 12 × 7½ inches, in center of first tier. Place fifth layer on cardboard; frost top. Place sixth layer directly on top of fifth; frost sides and top. Place aluminum foil-covered cardboard rectangle, 8 × 5½ inches, in center of second tier. Cut seventh layer crosswise into halves. Place half of the layer on cardboard; frost top. Place remaining half layer directly on top; frost sides and top.

Prepare Chocolate Decorator Frosting. Place in decorating bag with petal tip #104. Make about 30 chocolate roses of varying sizes (see page 10). Prepare Chocolate Leaves. Pipe leaf border around top edge, base and onto corners of all tiers with Chocolate Decorator Frosting and leaf tip #352. Arrange roses and leaves on cake as desired. About 168 servings, 2 × 1 inch.

Marble Cake

1¾ cups sugar	1¼ cups milk
⅔ cup margarine or butter, softened	2 ounces melted unsweetened chocolate (cool)
1½ teaspoons vanilla	1 tablespoon sugar
2 eggs	2 tablespoons warm water
2¾ cups all-purpose flour	
2½ teaspoons baking powder	¼ teaspoon baking soda
1 teaspoon salt	

Heat oven to 350°. Grease and flour rectangular pan, 13 × 9 × 2 inches. Beat 1¾ cups sugar, the margarine, vanilla and eggs in large bowl on medium speed, scraping bowl constantly, until blended, about 30 seconds. Beat on high speed, scraping bowl occasionally, 5 minutes. Beat in flour, baking powder and salt alternately with milk on medium speed.

Pour half of the batter into another bowl; stir in chocolate, 1 tablespoon sugar, the water and baking soda. Spoon batters alternately into pan. Cut through batter several times for marbled effect.

Bake until wooden pick inserted in center comes out clean, 40 to 45 minutes. Cool 10 minutes; remove from pan. Cool completely. Slice off rounded top for ease in stacking.

Coffee Cream Frosting

2 tablespoons instant powdered coffee	5⅓ cups powdered sugar
3 tablespoons water	⅔ cup margarine or butter, softened

Stir instant coffee into water until dissolved. Beat coffee mixture, powdered sugar and margarine on medium speed until frosting is smooth and spreading consistency. If necessary, stir in additional water, 1 teaspoon at a time.

Chocolate Decorator Frosting

2⅔ cups powdered sugar	2 ounces melted unsweetened chocolate (cool)
⅔ cup shortening	
	2 tablespoons water

Beat all ingredients on medium speed until frosting is smooth and desired consistency. If necessary, stir in additional water, ½ teaspoon at a time.

Chocolate Leaves

Wash and dry 12 to 18 leaves (such as rose leaves). Heat ½ cup semisweet chocolate chips or 2 squares (1 ounce each) semisweet chocolate and 1 teaspoon shortening over low heat until melted. Spread chocolate about ⅛ inch thick over backs of leaves. Refrigerate until firm, at least 1 hour. Peel off leaves. Refrigerate until ready to use.

○ Time-saver Tip: Substitute 7 packages (20 ounces each) marble cake mix with pudding for the Marble Cakes. Prepare and bake as directed on the package.

Petits Fours

Silver White Cake (below)   Decorator Frosting (below)
Petits Fours Glaze (below)

Bake Silver White Cake as directed. Cut cake into small squares, rounds, diamonds or hearts. Place cakes, one at a time, on wire rack over large bowl. Pour enough Petits Fours Glaze over top to cover top and sides. (Glaze can be reheated and used again.) Place Decorator Frosting in decorating bag with writing tip #3. Decorate as desired. 54 servings, 1½-inch square.

Silver White Cake

2¼ cups all-purpose flour   1 teaspoon salt
1⅔ cups sugar   1 teaspoon almond
 ⅔ cup shortening   extract
1¼ cups milk   5 egg whites
3½ teaspoons baking
   powder

Heat oven to 350°. Grease and flour jelly roll pan, 15½ × 10½ × 1 inch. Beat flour, sugar, shortening, milk, baking powder, salt and almond extract in large bowl on medium speed, scraping bowl constantly, until blended, about 30 seconds. Beat on high speed, scraping bowl occasionally, 2 minutes. Beat in egg whites on high speed, scraping bowl occasionally, 2 minutes. Pour into pan.

Bake until wooden pick inserted in center comes out clean, 25 to 30 minutes. Cool completely.

Petits Fours Glaze

8 cups powdered sugar   2 teaspoons almond
½ cup water   extract
½ cup light corn syrup

Mix all ingredients in top of double boiler until smooth. Heat just until lukewarm; remove from heat. Let glaze remain over hot water to prevent thickening. If necessary, add hot water, a few drops at a time, for desired consistency.

Decorator Frosting

Mix 2 cups powdered sugar and 2 to 3 tablespoons water — just enough to make a frosting that can be used easily in a decorating bag or envelope cone and yet hold its shape. Tint portions of frosting delicate pastel shades with food color if desired.

Petits Fours

Square Tiered Wedding Cake (page 60)

Square Tiered Wedding Cake

This cake could also be used for a large wedding anniversary celebration.

For this cake prepare 1 recipe Date Cake, 4 recipes Almond Pound Cake and 2½ recipes Creamy White Frosting (2 recipes to frost cake and pipe borders and ½ recipe for flowers and leaves.) Bake cake layers ahead of time and freeze or bake the day before they are to be assembled.

Date Cake (right)	Yellow and green food
Almond Pound Cake	color
(right)	1 tablespoon powdered
Creamy White Frosting	sugar
(right)	⅔ cup apricot preserves
¼ cup powdered sugar	

Prepare Date Cake as directed. Prepare Almond Pound Cake as directed; repeat 2 times. For the 4th recipe, grease and flour 2 square pans, 8 × 8 × 2 inches. Prepare Almond Pound Cake as directed except divide batter between pans. Bake in 350° oven until wooden pick inserted in center comes out clean, 25 to 30 minutes.

Prepare ½ recipe Creamy White Frosting. Stir ¼ cup powdered sugar into 1 cup of the frosting; tint yellow with 3 drops yellow food color (color will deepen slightly after storage). Make about 5 dozen marigolds (see page 10) with petal tip #101; place on waxed paper-lined cookie sheets to dry.

Stir 1 tablespoon powdered sugar into ¼ cup of the frosting; tint pale green with 1 drop green food color. Make about 5 dozen leaves (see page 9) with leaf tip #352; place on waxed paper-lined cookie sheets to dry.

When ready to assemble cake, heat apricot preserves slightly, stirring occasionally; strain. Refrigerate glaze.

To assemble cake: Place one 13 × 9 × 2-inch layer top side down on 15-inch square tray, mirror or large serving plate. Cut second 13 × 9 × 2-inch layer lengthwise into halves, making 2 halves, 13 × 4½ inches (see diagram 1). Place one half top side down against long side of layer on tray (see diagram 2).

Join parts of cake on tray with Creamy White Frosting; frost top. Spread ¼ cup apricot glaze thinly on frosting. Place remaining 13 × 9 × 2-inch layer and 13 × 4½ inch layer top sides up on filling (see diagram 3). Join parts with frosting; frost sides and top.

Place one 8-inch layer top side down on aluminum foil-covered 7-inch square of cardboard; frost top of layer. Spread thin layer of apricot glaze on frosting. Place remaining layer on top; trim top to make level if necessary (see diagram 4). Frost sides and top of tier. Place frosted tier (with cardboard base) on center of cake on tray.

Cut Date Cake crosswise into halves, making 2 halves, 8 × 4 inches. Cut one half into two 4-inch squares; trim to make level if necessary. Place one square upside down on aluminum foil-covered 3½-inch square of cardboard; frost top of square. Spread thin layer of apricot glaze on frosting. Place remaining square on top. Frost sides and top of tier. Place frosted tier (with cardboard base) on center of cake on tray (for a different effect, place tier diagonally on cake). Use remaining Date Cake as desired.

Pipe shell border around top edge, base and onto corners of all tiers with open star tip #32. Place small mound (1 to 2 tablespoons) frosting on top tier. Arrange marigolds and leaves on top and sides of cake as desired. (Use small dab of frosting to attach flowers and leaves.) About 70 servings, 2 × 1½ inches.

Date Cake

1⅔ cups all-purpose flour	1 teaspoon vanilla
1 cup sugar	1 egg
¼ cup shortening	1 cup cut-up dates*
1 cup water	½ cup finely chopped
1 teaspoon baking soda	almonds
½ teaspoon salt	

Heat oven to 350°. Grease and flour square pan, 8 × 8 × 2 inches. Beat all ingredients in large bowl on medium speed, scraping bowl constantly, until blended, 30 seconds. Beat on high speed, scraping bowl occasionally, 3 minutes. Pour into pan.

Bake until wooden pick inserted in center comes out clean, 45 to 50 minutes. Cool 10 minutes; remove from pan. Cool completely.

*Packaged sugar-coated chopped dates can be substituted for the cut-up dates.

Almond Pound Cake

2 cups all-purpose flour	3 teaspoons baking
1 cup sugar	powder
1/4 cup shortening	1 teaspoon salt
1/4 cup margarine or	1 teaspoon almond extract
butter, softened	1 teaspoon vanilla
3/4 cup milk	2 eggs

Heat oven to 350°. Grease and flour rectangular pan, 13 × 9 × 2 inches. Beat all ingredients in large bowl on medium speed, scraping bowl constantly, until blended, about 30 seconds. Beat on high speed, scraping bowl occasionally, 3 minutes. Pour into pan.

Bake until wooden pick inserted in center comes out clean, 30 to 35 minutes. Cool 10 minutes; remove from pan. Cool completely.

Creamy White Frosting

8 cups powdered sugar	1 1/2 teaspoons almond
1/2 cup shortening	extract
1/4 cup margarine or	1/2 cup milk
butter, softened	

Beat all ingredients on medium speed until smooth and spreading consistency. If necessary, stir in additional milk, 1 teaspoon at a time.

○ *Time-saver Tip:* Substitute 4 packages (16 ounces each) golden pound cake mix for the Almond Pound Cakes. Prepare as directed on package except add 1 teaspoon almond extract before beating. Bake in 13 × 9 × 2-inch pan at 325° until top springs back when touched lightly, 35 to 40 minutes.

Cutting and Assembling Square Tiered Wedding Cake

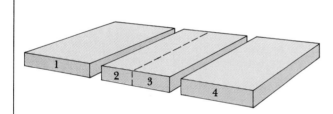

Place one 13 × 9 × 2-inch layer on tray. Cut second layer lengthwise into halves (leave third layer uncut).

Place one half against long side of layer on tray; frost and glaze. (See page 13 for use of dowels in assembling.) Place remaining 13 × 9 × 2-inch layer and 13 × 4½-inch layer on filling; frost as directed.

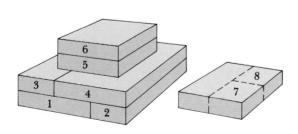

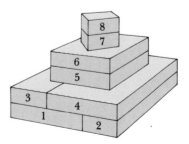

Place one 8-inch layer on cardboard; frost and glaze. Place remaining layer on top; frost. Place on bottom tier.

Fill and frost two 4-inch squares of Date Cake; place on middle tier.

Chocolate Tiered Cake

Custom-tailor decorations and color scheme of this versatile cake for any large gathering—an anniversary, reunion or graduation party; or serve as an elegant groom's cake for a wedding reception.

For this cake prepare 3 recipes Dark Chocolate Cake, 4 recipes Chocolate Butter Frosting and 1 recipe Buttercream Frosting. Make the flowers several days ahead of time. Bake the cake layers the day before assembling or bake ahead and freeze.

Dark Chocolate Cake (right)	*Buttercream Frosting (right)*
Chocolate Butter Frosting (right)	*Red and yellow food color*

Bake Dark Chocolate Cake as directed. Repeat for second and third layers. Prepare Chocolate Butter Frosting, repeating as necessary. Place 1 cake layer upside down on tray, mirror or large serving plate, about 16 × 12 inches. Frost top of cake with ¾ cup of the frosting. Add second layer, top side up. Frost sides and top with 2½ cups of the frosting. Place aluminum foil-covered cardboard, 8 × 4 inches, in center of tier.

Cut third layer crosswise into 3 rectangles, 8 × 4 inches each. Use 2 rectangles for middle tier of cake, trimming tops to make level if necessary. Fill layers and frost cut sides and top before placing on cake to prevent crumbs on bottom layer. Place middle layers on aluminum foil-covered cardboard; frost remaining sides.

Cut remaining 8 × 4-inch rectangle crosswise into halves. Use for top tier of cake, trimming top and sides to make level and in proportion to other tiers if necessary. Fill layers; frost cut sides and top. Place on cake; frost remaining sides.

Place Chocolate Butter Frosting in decorating bag with open star tip #32. Pipe rope border (see page 9) around base, top edge and on corners of each tier. Using same tip or star tip #18, pipe straight lines in diagonal design on sides, reserving ⅔ cup frosting for bases of flower clusters.

Prepare Buttercream Frosting; reserve ½ cup. Using petal tip #104 make as many wild roses (see page 10) as desired; place on waxed paper-lined cookie sheets to dry. Tint reserved frosting salmon pink with 3 drops red food color and 2 drops yellow food color for additional flowers. Make dots in contrasting colors for the centers of each flower with writing tip #3.

Mound about ⅓ cup of the reserved chocolate frosting on top of cake; arrange flowers as desired on top. Mound about 1 teaspoon of the chocolate frosting on center of each corner of middle tier; arrange flowers on mounds and cascade along sides as desired. Mound about 1 tablespoon of the chocolate frosting on center of each corner of bottom tier; arrange flowers as desired. 50 servings, 2 × 1½ inches.

Dark Chocolate Cake

2 cups all-purpose flour or cake flour	1 teaspoon salt
2 cups sugar	½ teaspoon baking powder
½ cup shortening	4 ounces melted unsweetened chocolate (cool)
¾ cup water	
¾ cup buttermilk	
1 teaspoon baking soda	2 eggs

Heat oven to 350°. Grease and flour rectangular pan, 13 × 9 × 2 inches. Beat all ingredients in large bowl on medium speed, scraping bowl constantly, until blended, about 30 seconds. Beat on high speed, scraping bowl occasionally, 3 minutes. Pour into pan.

Bake until wooden pick inserted in center comes out clean, 35 to 40 minutes. Cool 10 minutes; remove from pan. Cool completely.

Chocolate Butter Frosting

5½ cups powdered sugar	⅓ cup cocoa
½ cup margarine or butter, softened	1½ teaspoons vanilla
½ cup shortening	¼ cup water

Beat all ingredients on medium speed until smooth and spreading consistency. If necessary, stir in additional water, 1 teaspoon at a time.

Buttercream Frosting

3 cups powdered sugar	¼ cup shortening
¼ cup margarine or butter, softened	1 tablespoon water
	½ teaspoon vanilla

Beat all ingredients on medium speed until frosting is smooth and desired consistency. If necessary, stir in additional powdered sugar. (Roses may need additional powdered sugar.)

○ *Time-saver Tip:* Substitute 3 packages (18.5 ounces each) devils food cake mix with pudding for the Dark Chocolate Cakes. Prepare and bake as directed on package.

Chocolate Tiered Cake

Cutting and Assembling Chocolate Tiered Cake

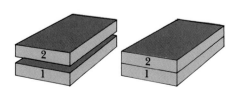

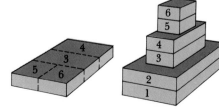

Place 1 cake layer on tray; frost top. (See page 13 for use of dowels in assembling.) Add second layer; trim top to make level if necessary. Frost sides and top.

Cut third layer crosswise into 3 rectangles, 8 × 4 inches each. Fill and frost cut sides of 2 rectangles; place on bottom tier. Frost remaining sides. Cut remaining rectangle crosswise into halves. Fill and frost cut sides and top. Place on middle tier, frost remaining sides.

Double Ring Cake

Silver White Cake (below)
Fluffy Decorator Frosting
  (right)
½ cup sifted powdered
  sugar

Bake Silver White Cake as directed. Place cakes side by side, edges touching, on large tray or aluminum foil-covered cardboard, about 24 × 14 inches. Reserve 2 cups Fluffy Decorator Frosting for decorating; frost cakes with remaining frosting.

Fold powdered sugar into reserved frosting. Place in decorating bag with star tip #32. Pipe swag border around top and bottom edge of rings (see page 9) or other designs as desired. 32 servings.

Silver White Cake

2¼ cups all-purpose flour
1⅔ cups sugar
⅔ cup shortening
1¼ cups milk
3½ teaspoons baking
  powder
1 teaspoon salt
1 teaspoon vanilla
5 egg whites

Heat oven to 350°. Grease and flour 12-cup ring mold. Beat flour, sugar, shortening, milk, baking powder, salt and vanilla in large bowl on medium speed, scraping bowl constantly, until blended, about 30 seconds. Beat on high speed, scraping bowl occasionally, 2 minutes. Beat in egg whites on high speed, scraping bowl occasionally, 2 minutes. Pour into pan.

Bake until wooden pick inserted in center comes out clean, 35 to 40 minutes. Cool 10 minutes; remove from pan. Cool completely. Repeat for second ring.

Fluffy Decorator Frosting

1 cup granulated
  sugar
½ cup light corn syrup
¼ cup water
4 egg whites
1 teaspoon almond
  extract
4 cups sifted powdered
  sugar

Mix granulated sugar, corn syrup and water in 1-quart saucepan. Cover and heat to rolling boil over medium heat. Uncover and boil rapidly until candy thermometer registers 242° or until small amount of mixture dropped into very cold water forms a firm ball that holds its shape until pressed.

As mixture boils, beat egg whites in large bowl just until stiff peaks form. Pour hot syrup very slowly in a thin stream into egg whites, beating constantly on medium speed. Add almond extract; beat on high speed until stiff peaks form. Beat in powdered sugar, 1 cup at a time, on low speed.

NOTE: For best results in cake decorating of this type, sifted powdered sugar is recommended for use in the frosting.

○ *Time-saver Tip:* Substitute 2 packages (18.5 ounces each) white cake mix with pudding for the Silver White Cakes. Prepare and bake as directed on package. Substitute 2 packages (7.2 ounces each) fluffy white frosting mix for the Fluffy Decorator Frosting. Prepare as directed on package except use 1 cup boiling water. Beat in large mixer bowl until soft peaks form, 5 to 7 minutes. Beat in 1 teaspoon almond extract and 4 cups powdered sugar, 1 cup at a time, on low speed.

Double Ring Cake

Almond Petal Cake

Almond Petal Cake

Bonnie Butter Cake
(below)
Toasted Almond
Filling (right)
1 1/2 cups chilled whipping
cream

1/2 cup powdered sugar
1/2 teaspoon almond
extract
Red food color,
if desired

Bake Bonnie Butter Cake as directed. Fill layers with Toasted Almond Filling. Beat whipping cream and powdered sugar in chilled bowl until stiff; add almond extract during last few seconds of beating. Tint pink with 2 or 3 drops food color.

To frost cake with petal design, use about 1 teaspoon frosting on tip of spatula for each petal. Beginning at base of cake, form petals by pressing spatula with frosting against side of cake. Form petals in rows around cake, overlapping petals slightly. Make larger petals on top of cake. Refrigerate any remaining cake. 14 to 16 servings.

Bonnie Butter Cake

2 3/4 cups all-purpose flour
1 3/4 cups sugar
2/3 cup margarine or
butter, softened
1 1/4 cups milk

2 1/2 teaspoons baking
powder
1 teaspoon salt
1 1/2 teaspoons vanilla
2 eggs

Heat oven to 350°. Grease and flour 2 round pans, 9 × 1 1/2 inches, or 3 round pans, 8 × 1 1/2 inches. Beat all ingredients in large bowl on medium speed, scraping bowl constantly, until blended, about 30 seconds. Beat on high speed, scraping bowl occasionally, 3 minutes. Pour into pans.

Bake until wooden pick inserted in center comes out clean, 30 to 35 minutes. Cool 10 minutes; remove from pans. Cool completely.

Toasted Almond Filling

1/2 cup packed brown
sugar
2 tablespoons margarine
or butter

2 tablespoons water
1 egg yolk, slightly beaten
1/2 cup toasted sliced
almonds

Heat brown sugar, margarine and water in 1-quart saucepan to boiling, stirring constantly. Stir at least half of the hot mixture gradually into egg yolk; blend into hot mixture in saucepan. Boil and stir 1 minute. Remove from heat; stir in almonds.

NOTE: To toast almonds, heat in 350° oven on ungreased cookie sheet until golden brown, stirring occasionally, 5 to 7 minutes.

○ Time-saver Tip: Substitute 1 package (18.5 ounces) white, yellow or devils food cake mix with pudding for the Bonnie Butter Cake. Prepare and bake as directed on the package for two 8- or 9-inch rounds.

Cupcake Petits Fours

Silver White Cupcakes   *Petits Fours Glaze (below)*
(below)   *Decorator Frosting (below)*

Bake Silver White Cupcakes as directed. Spread tops with Petits Fours Glaze. Place Decorator Frosting in decorating bag with writing tip #3. Decorate as desired. 2½ dozen cupcakes.

Silver White Cupcakes

2¼ cups all-purpose flour   1 teaspoon salt
1⅔ cups sugar   1 teaspoon almond
 ⅔ cup shortening   extract
1¼ cups milk   5 egg whites
3½ teaspoons baking
    powder

Heat oven to 350°. Beat flour, sugar, shortening, milk, baking powder, salt and almond extract in large bowl on medium speed, scraping bowl constantly, until blended, about 30 seconds. Beat on high speed, scraping bowl occasionally, 2 minutes. Beat in egg whites on high speed, scraping bowl occasionally, 2 minutes. Pour into paper-lined medium muffin cups, 2½ × 1¼ inches, filling each ½ full.

Bake until wooden pick inserted in center comes out clean, 20 to 25 minutes. Immediately remove from pan; cool completely.

Petits Fours Glaze

2 cups powdered sugar   ½ teaspoon almond
2 tablespoons water   extract
2 tablespoons light corn
    syrup

Beat all ingredients in saucepan until smooth. Heat over low heat just until lukewarm; remove from heat. If necessary, add hot water, a few drops at a time, until proper consistency.

Decorator Frosting

Mix 2 cups powdered sugar and 2 to 3 tablespoons water — just enough to make a frosting that can be used easily in a decorating bag or envelope cone and yet hold its shape. Tint portions of frosting delicate pastel shades with food color.

○ *Time-saver Tip:* Substitute 1 package (18.5 ounces) white cake mix with pudding for the Silver White Cupcakes. Prepare and bake as directed on package for cupcakes.

Umbrella Shower Cake

Silver White Cake (below)
Lemon Filling (below)

Fluffy Lemon Frosting
(right)
Fruit candy slices

Bake Silver White Cake as directed. Fill layers with Lemon Filling. Frost cake with Fluffy Lemon Frosting, making top smooth.

Cut 3 small V's from bottom of candy slice to make umbrella top. Cut "peel" from another candy slice and use for handle. Cut small piece off handle for tip of umbrella. Assemble as shown in diagram. Decorate top or side of cake with "umbrellas," 12 to 16 servings.

Silver White Cake

2¼ cups all-purpose flour
1²/₃ cups sugar
²/₃ cup shortening
1¼ cups milk
3½ teaspoons baking
    powder

1 teaspoon salt
1 teaspoon lemon
    extract
5 egg whites

Heat oven to 350°. Grease and flour 2 round pans, 9 × 1½ inches. Beat flour, sugar, shortening, milk, baking powder, salt and lemon extract in large bowl on medium speed, scraping bowl constantly, until blended, about 30 seconds. Beat on high speed, scraping bowl occasionally, 2 minutes. Beat in egg whites on high speed, scraping bowl occasionally, 2 minutes. Pour into pans.

Bake until wooden pick inserted in center comes out clean, 30 to 35 minutes. Cool 10 minutes; remove from pans. Cool completely.

Lemon Filling

¾ cup sugar
3 tablespoons cornstarch
¼ teaspoon salt
¾ cup water
1 teaspoon finely
    shredded lemon peel

1 tablespoon margarine
    or butter
1/3 cup lemon juice
2 drops yellow food color

Mix sugar, cornstarch and salt in saucepan. Stir in water gradually. Cook, stirring constantly, until mixture thickens and boils. Boil and stir 5 minutes. Remove from heat; add lemon peel and margarine. Stir in lemon juice and food color; cool. If filling is too soft, refrigerate until set.

Fluffy Lemon Frosting

½ cup sugar
¼ cup light corn syrup
2 tablespoons water
2 egg whites

¼ teaspoon finely
    shredded lemon peel
1 tablespoon lemon juice
6 to 8 drops yellow food
    color

Mix sugar, corn syrup and water in saucepan. Cover and heat to rolling boil over medium heat. Uncover and boil rapidly until candy thermometer registers 242° or until small amount of mixture dropped into very cold water forms a firm ball that holds its shape until pressed.

As mixture boils, beat egg whites until stiff peaks form. Pour hot syrup very slowly in a thin stream into egg whites, beating constantly on medium speed. Beat on high speed until stiff peaks form. Beat in lemon peel, lemon juice and food color.

○ *Time-saver Tip:* Substitute 1 package (18.5 ounces) white cake mix with pudding for the Silver White Cake. Prepare and bake as directed on package. Substitute 1 package (7.2 ounces) fluffy white frosting mix for the Fluffy Lemon Frosting. Prepare as directed on package except stir in 1 tablespoon finely shredded lemon peel and 6 to 8 drops yellow food color.

Umbrella Preparation

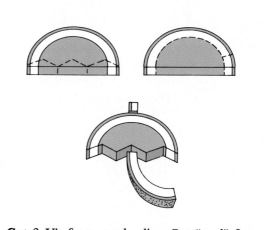

Cut 3 V's from candy slice. Cut "peel" for handle from another slice. Cut piece off handle for tip.

Baby's Bib Cake

Almond Cake (below)   Red and blue food color
Creamy Almond Frosting
    (below)

Bake Almond Cake as directed. Reserve 1 cup Creamy Almond Frosting for decorating. Fill and frost cake with remaining frosting. Make vertical lines on side of cake with decorating comb or tines of fork if desired.

Tint ⅔ cup of the reserved frosting pink with 1 or 2 drops red food color. Place pink frosting in decorating bag with small writing tip #2. Pipe 2 circles around outer top edge of cake, about 1 inch apart, leaving 3-inch opening at top. Make loop design within circles.

Tint remaining frosting blue with 1 or 2 drops blue food color. Place blue frosting in decorating bag with writing tip #5; pipe outer border of bib. Pipe inner opening of bib about 3 inches in diameter; join circles with tie at top. Make small bows on bib and write desired message in bib opening. Pipe dots between bows with remaining pink frosting if desired. 12 to 16 servings.

Almond Cake

2 cups all-purpose flour	3½ teaspoons baking
1½ cups sugar	powder
½ cup shortening (half	1 teaspoon salt
margarine or butter,	1 teaspoon vanilla
softened, if desired)	½ teaspoon almond
1 cup milk	extract
	3 eggs

Heat oven to 350°. Grease and flour 2 round pans, 8 or 9 × 1½ inches. Beat all ingredients in large bowl on medium speed, scraping bowl constantly, until blended, about 30 seconds. Beat on high speed, scraping bowl occasionally, 3 minutes. Pour into pans.

Bake until wooden pick inserted in center comes out clean, 30 to 35 minutes. Cool 10 minutes; remove from pans. Cool completely.

Creamy Almond Frosting

4½ cups powdered sugar	1½ teaspoons almond
½ cup shortening	extract
	⅓ cup milk

Beat all ingredients on medium speed until smooth and spreading consistency. If necessary, stir in additional milk, ½ teaspoon at a time.

Clockwise from left: Baby's Bib Cake, Umbrella Shower Cake (page 67), Baby's Booties (page 70)

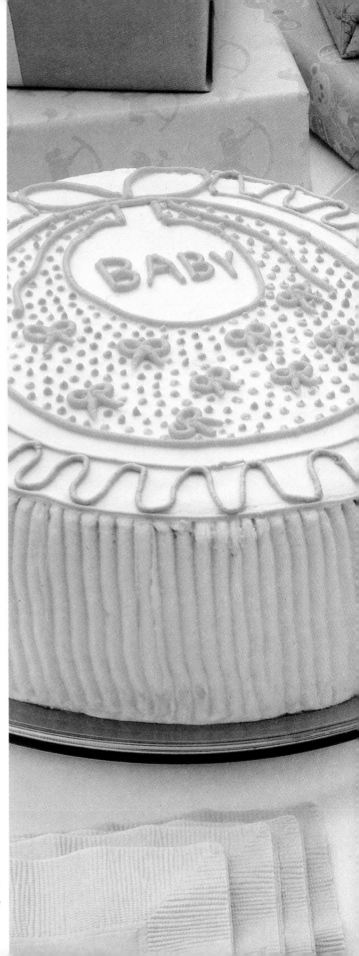

Baby's Booties

Silver White Cupcakes
(below)
White Mountain Frosting
(page 16)

Miniature Marshmallows
Gumdrops

Bake Silver White Cupcakes as directed. Remove paper baking cups. Place 2 cupcakes upside down on separate plates. Cut small piece off side of a third cupcake to form flat surface. Cut third cupcake horizontally into halves; place one half with cut side against cupcake on plate as shown in diagram. Place remaining half against second cupcake. Repeat with remaining cupcakes.

Tint White Mountain Frosting with food color if desired. Frost cupcake booties, joining toe to cupcake with frosting. Decorate booties with miniature marshmallows and bows made from rolled gumdrops. 20 booties (2½ dozen cupcakes).

Silver White Cupcakes

2¼ cups all-purpose flour
1⅔ cups sugar
⅔ cup shortening
1¼ cups milk

3½ teaspoons baking
   powder
1 teaspoon salt
1 teaspoon vanilla
5 egg whites

Heat oven to 350°. Beat flour, sugar, shortening, milk, baking powder, salt and vanilla in large bowl on medium speed, scraping bowl constantly, until blended, about 30 seconds. Beat on high speed, scraping bowl occasionally, 2 minutes. Beat in egg whites on high speed, scraping bowl occasionally, 2 minutes. Pour into paper-lined medium muffin cups, 2½ × 1¼ inches, filling each ½ full.

Bake until wooden pick inserted in center comes out clean, 20 to 25 minutes. Immediately remove from pan; cool completely.

○ *Time-saver Tip:* Substitute 1 package (18.5 ounces) white cake mix with pudding for the Silver White Cupcakes. Prepare and bake as directed on package for cupcakes. Substitute 1 package (7.2 ounces) fluffy white frosting mix for the White Mountain Frosting. Prepare as directed on the package.

Cutting and Assembling Booties

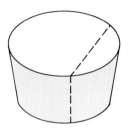

Cut piece off side of 1 cupcake.

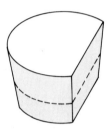

Cut cupcake horizontally into halves.

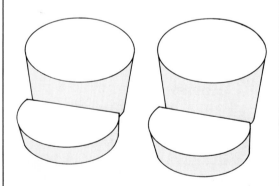

Place halves with cut sides against 2 other cupcakes.

Birthday Cupcakes

These candleholder ideas can be adapted easily to layer cakes.

Starlight Cupcakes (below)	2 tablespoons cocoa, if desired
Vanilla Butter Frosting (right)	Ring-shaped hard candies*
	Small birthday candles

Bake Starlight Cupcakes as directed. Mix cocoa into half of the Vanilla Butter Frosting. Frost half of the cupcakes with plain frosting and half with cocoa frosting. Place a hard candy on each cupcake; insert candle into each. 3 dozen cupcakes.

*Other suggestions for candleholders:

1. Circle of 5 colored marshmallows or pastel pillow mints
2. Circle of red cinnamon candies
3. Red or green maraschino cherry (press candle into hole of stem end)
4. Large gumdrop (snip top portion into 5 or 6 petals; pull petals apart)
5. Large marshmallow and green gumdrop (snip marshmallow into 5 sections, insert candle and place on cupcake; snip gumdrop into pieces for stem and leaves)

Starlight Cupcakes

2 cups all-purpose flour	3½ teaspoons baking
1½ cups sugar	powder
½ cup shortening (half margarine or butter, softened, if desired)	1 teaspoon salt
	1 teaspoon vanilla
	3 eggs
1 cup milk	

Heat oven to 350°. Beat all ingredients in large bowl on medium speed, scraping bowl constantly, until blended, about 30 seconds. Beat on high speed, scraping bowl occasionally, 3 minutes. Pour into paper-lined medium muffin cups, 2½ × 1¼ inches, filling each ½ full.

Bake until wooden pick inserted in center comes out clean, 20 to 25 minutes. Immediately remove from pans. Cool completely.

Vanilla Butter Frosting

3 cups powdered sugar	1½ teaspoons vanilla
⅓ cup margarine or butter, softened	2 tablespoons milk

Beat all ingredients on medium speed until smooth and spreading consistency. If necessary, stir in additional milk, ½ teaspoon at a time.

○ *Time-saver Tip:* Substitute 1 package (18.5 ounces) yellow cake mix with pudding for the Starlight Cupcakes. Prepare and bake as directed on package for cupcakes. Substitute 1 package (14.3 ounces) creamy white frosting mix for the Vanilla Butter Frosting. Prepare as directed on package.

Birthday Cupcakes

Fiesta Birthday Cake

Pastel Marble Cake (below)
Vanilla Butter Frosting
 (below)

Red and green food color

Bake Pastel Marble Cake as directed. Reserve 1¼ cups Vanilla Butter Frosting for decorating. Frost cake with remaining frosting. Place ⅔ cup of the reserved frosting in decorating bag with star tip #18; pipe zigzag lines on cake to divide into 15 servings and make borders around top and bottom edge of cake.

Tint ½ cup of the reserved frosting pink with 2 to 4 drops red food color; make drop flowers (see page 8) on all servings. Tint remaining frosting green with 1 drop green food color; pipe leaves on flowers with leaf tip #352. 15 servings.

Pastel Marble Cake

2¼ cups cake flour	1 teaspoon salt
1½ cups sugar	½ teaspoon baking soda
½ cup shortening (half	1 teaspoon vanilla
margarine or butter,	2 eggs
softened)	Red and green food
1 cup buttermilk	color
1½ teaspoons baking	
powder	

Heat oven to 350°. Grease and flour rectangular pan, 13 × 9 × 2 inches. Beat all ingredients except food color in large bowl on medium speed, scraping bowl constantly, until blended, about 30 seconds. Beat on high speed, scraping bowl occasionally, 3 minutes. Divide batter into 3 equal parts. Tint ⅓ pink with 2 or 3 drops red food color and tint ⅓ green with 2 or 3 drops green food color. Drop batter by alternate color spoonfuls into pan.

Bake until wooden pick inserted in center comes out clean, 40 to 45 minutes. Cool 10 minutes; remove from pan. Cool completely.

Vanilla Butter Frosting

5½ cups powdered sugar	1 teaspoon vanilla
⅔ cup margarine or	3 tablespoons milk
butter, softened	

Beat all ingredients on medium speed until smooth and spreading consistency. If necessary, stir in additional milk, 1 teaspoon at a time.

○ *Time-saver Tip:* Substitute 1 package (18.5 ounces) white or yellow cake mix with pudding for the Pastel Marble Cake. Prepare and bake as directed on package except tint batter and spoon into pan as directed above.

Fiesta Birthday Cake, left, Confetti Party Cakes, right

Confetti Party Cakes

Confetti Angel Food   Creamy Glaze (below)
Loaves (below)   Decorator Frosting (below)

Bake Confetti Angel Food Loaves as directed. Spread loaves with Creamy Glaze. Place Decorator Frosting in decorating bag with writing tip #3. Pipe names across each serving and decorate base or, if desired, sprinkle one loaf with confetti candy bits. 16 servings.

Confetti Angel Food Loaves

1 cup cake flour	³⁄₄ cup sugar
³⁄₄ cup plus 2 tablespoons sugar	¹⁄₄ teaspoon salt
1¹⁄₂ cups egg whites (about 12)	1¹⁄₂ teaspoons vanilla
	¹⁄₂ teaspoon almond extract
1¹⁄₂ teaspoons cream of tartar	¹⁄₄ cup confetti candy bits

Heat oven to 375°. Mix flour and ³⁄₄ cup plus 2 tablespoons sugar. Beat egg whites and cream of tartar in large bowl on medium speed until foamy. Beat in ³⁄₄ cup sugar on high speed, 2 tablespoons at a time; continue beating until stiff and glossy. Add salt, vanilla and almond extract with the last addition of sugar. Beat in candy bits on low speed about 15 seconds.

Sprinkle flour-sugar mixture, ¹⁄₄ cup at a time, over meringue, folding in just until flour-sugar mixture disappears. Divide batter between 2 ungreased loaf pans, 9 × 5 × 3 inches. Cut gently through batter with metal spatula.

Bake until cracks feel dry and top springs back when touched lightly, 30 to 35 minutes. Invert pans with edges on 2 other pans; let hang until loaves are cold. Remove from pans.

Creamy Glaze

²⁄₃ cup margarine or butter	2 teaspoons almond extract
4 cups powdered sugar	¹⁄₄ to ¹⁄₂ cup hot water

Heat margarine in saucepan until melted. Stir in powdered sugar and almond extract. Stir in water, about 1 tablespoon at a time, until glaze is desired consistency.

Decorator Frosting

Mix 2 cups powdered sugar, few drops green food color and 2 to 3 tablespoons water—just enough to make a frosting that can be used easily in a decorating bag or envelope cone and yet hold its shape.

○ *Time-saver Tip:* Substitute 1 package (16 ounces) white angel food cake mix for the Confetti Angel Food Loaves. Prepare as directed on package. Bake as directed above for loaves.

Rose Birthday Cake

Write your own message for Mother's Day or a small anniversary celebration; tint roses yellow or a favorite color.

Cherry Cake (below)	Red and green food
Buttercream Decorator	color
Frosting (right)	¼ cup powdered sugar

Bake Cherry Cake as directed. Reserve 1¾ cups Buttercream Decorator Frosting for decorating. Fill and frost cake with remaining frosting. Tint ⅔ cup of the reserved frosting pink with 5 to 7 drops red food color. Mix ½ cup of the pink frosting with powdered sugar; make 3 to 5 roses (see page 10). Place roses on cake.

Tint ⅓ cup of the reserved frosting green with 3 to 5 drops green food color. Pipe stems and leaves (see page 9) as desired to form spray effect on top of cake. Use remaining pink frosting and writing tip #5 to write desired message on cake. Pipe shell border around base and top edge of cake with remaining white frosting and open star tip #32. 12 to 16 servings.

Cherry Cake

2 cups all-purpose flour	1 teaspoon salt
1½ cups sugar	1 teaspoon vanilla
½ cup shortening (half	3 eggs
margarine or butter,	½ cup finely chopped
softened, if desired)	maraschino cherries,
1 cup milk	well drained
3½ teaspoons baking	
powder	

Heat oven to 350°. Grease and flour 2 round pans, 8 or 9×1½ inches. Beat all ingredients in large bowl on medium speed, scraping bowl constantly, until blended, about 30 seconds. Beat on high speed, scraping bowl occasionally, 3 minutes. Pour into pans.

Bake until wooden pick inserted in center comes out clean, 30 to 35 minutes. Cool 10 minutes; remove from pans. Cool completely.

Buttercream Decorator Frosting

6 cups powdered sugar	3 tablespoons water
¾ cup margarine or	1½ teaspoons almond
butter, softened	extract
¾ cup shortening	

Beat all ingredients on medium speed until frosting is smooth and desired consistency. If necessary, stir in additional powdered sugar. (Roses may need additional powdered sugar.)

○ Time-saver Tip: Substitute 1 package (18.5 ounces) yellow cake mix with pudding for the Cherry Cake. Prepare and bake as directed on package except fold ½ cup finely chopped maraschino cherries, well drained, into batter.

SUGARED ROSES

Beat 1 egg white with 1 teaspoon water just until foamy. Trim stems of small washed roses (see Fresh Flower Decorations, page 90) to about 2 inches. Brush egg white mixture on rose petals with a small, soft brush, separating petals as you coat them. Sift or sprinkle superfine or granulated sugar lightly on roses, shaking gently to remove excess sugar. Leaves can be sugared in the same manner if desired. Place on foil-lined tray to dry 1 to 3 days, turning once or twice a day. Arrange roses and leaves on cake. Other flowers that can be sugared are violets, sweet peas, small orchids, carnations, bachelor buttons and chrysanthemums. (These flowers are for decorating only.)

Butterfly Cakes

Orange-Coconut Cake
  (below)
Orange Fluffy Frosting
  (right)

1 ounce melted
   unsweetened
   chocolate (cool)
   Black shoestring
   licorice

Bake Orange-Coconut Cake as directed. Cut each layer vertically into halves; cut a notch on each cut side, slightly below center, to form wings as shown in diagram. For each butterfly, arrange 2 "wings" on a tray, 14 × 10 inches; use 2 of the leftover notched pieces to form the body, trimming if necessary. Frost butterflies with Orange Fluffy Frosting.

Using a teaspoon, carefully drizzle chocolate on frosting in 2 parallel lines along straight sides; immediately draw spatula or knife through lines at right angles, alternating directions, to form shadow pattern as shown. Frost bodies of butterflies with melted chocolate and add markings on wings if desired. Add licorice strips for antennae. 2 butterfly cakes (7 or 8 servings each).

Orange-Coconut Cake

  2 cups all-purpose flour
1½ cups sugar
  1 cup flaked coconut
 ½ cup shortening (half
     margarine or butter,
     softened, if desired)
  1 cup milk

3½ teaspoons baking
     powder
  1 tablespoon finely
     shredded orange
     peel
  1 teaspoon salt
  1 teaspoon vanilla
  3 eggs

Heat oven to 350°. Grease and flour 2 round pans, 9 × 1½ inches. Beat all ingredients in large bowl on medium speed, scraping bowl constantly, until blended, 30 seconds. Beat on high speed, scraping bowl occasionally, 3 minutes. Pour into pans.

Bake until wooden pick inserted in center comes out clean, 30 to 35 minutes. Cool 10 minutes; remove from pans. Cool completely.

Orange Fluffy Frosting

½ cup sugar
¼ cup light corn syrup
2 tablespoons water
2 egg whites

1 teaspoon finely
   shredded orange peel
4 drops yellow food color
1 or 2 drops red food
   color

Mix sugar, corn syrup and water in 1-quart saucepan. Cover and heat to rolling boil over medium heat. Uncover and boil rapidly until candy thermometer registers 242° or until small amount of mixture dropped into very cold water forms a firm ball that holds its shape until pressed.

As mixture boils, beat egg whites in small bowl just until stiff peaks form. Pour hot syrup very slowly in thin stream into egg whites, beating constantly on medium speed. Beat on high speed until stiff. Fold in orange peel and food color.

○ Time-saver Tip: Substitute 1 package (18.5 ounces) yellow cake mix with pudding for the Orange-Coconut Cake. Prepare and bake as directed on package except stir 1 tablespoon finely shredded orange peel and 1 cup flaked coconut into batter. Substitute 1 package (7.2 ounces) fluffy white frosting mix for the Orange Fluffy Frosting. Prepare as directed on package except fold in 1 teaspoon finely shredded orange peel and the food color after beating.

Cutting and Assembling Butterfly Cake

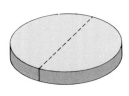  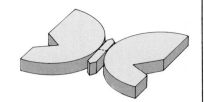

Cut each layer vertically into halves.

Cut notch on cut sides, slightly below center.

Arrange 2 "wings" on tray; use 2 notched pieces to form body.

Train Birthday Cake

Chocolate Loaf Cake (below)	Ring-shaped hard candy mints
Fudge Frosting (below)	Pastel mint wafers
	Shoestring licorice

Bake Chocolate Loaf Cake as directed. Frost loaves with Fudge Frosting. Arrange loaves on large tray or aluminum foil-covered cardboard, about 20 × 14 inches. Decorate with candy mints for wheels. Arrange mint wafers on top of each loaf to resemble balloons. Cut pieces of licorice for strings tied to balloons. 8 loaves.

Chocolate Loaf Cake

1½ cups all-purpose flour	½ teaspoon salt
1 cup sugar	1 teaspoon vanilla
¼ cup margarine or butter, softened	4 egg yolks
¼ cup shortening	2 ounces melted unsweetened chocolate (cool)
¾ cup milk	
2 teaspoons baking powder	

Heat oven to 350°. Grease and flour 8 small loaf pans, 4½ × 2¾ × 1¼ inches. Beat all ingredients in large bowl on medium speed, scraping bowl constantly, until blended, about 30 seconds. Beat on medium speed, scraping bowl occasionally, 3 minutes. Pour into pans, filling each ½ full.

Bake until wooden pick inserted in center comes out clean, 20 to 25 minutes. Cool 10 minutes; remove from pans. Cool completely.

NOTE: If loaf pans are not available, bake in square pan, 9 × 9 × 2 inches; cut into 4 × 2½-inch pieces. Frost and decorate as directed.

Fudge Frosting

1 package (6 ounces) semisweet chocolate chips	2 tablespoons margarine or butter
	3 cups powdered sugar
	⅓ cup milk

Heat chocolate chips and margarine over low heat, stirring constantly, until chocolate is melted. Beat in powdered sugar and milk until frosting is smooth and spreading consistency.

○ *Time-saver Tip:* Substitute 1 package (14.3 ounces) chocolate fudge frosting mix for the Fudge Frosting. Prepare as directed on package.

Corral Cake

Chocolate Fudge Cake (below)	Black licorice twists (6 or 7)
Chocolate-Peanut Butter Frosting (below)	Black shoestring licorice

Bake Chocolate Fudge Cake as directed. Fill and frost cake with Chocolate-Peanut Butter Frosting. Cut licorice twists crosswise into halves. Encircle side of cake with twists placed 2 to 3 inches apart for the posts and shoestring licorice 1½ inches apart for the wires. Weave "wires" under and over alternate "posts."

Write name and age of child on top of cake with small pieces of shoestring licorice. Make a circle around age with licorice. Small birthday candles placed at angles in a group make a "bonfire" if desired. To serve, use scissors to cut licorice "wires". Allow 1 licorice twist per serving. 12 to 14 servings.

Chocolate Fudge Cake

1⅔ cups all-purpose flour	1¼ teaspoons baking soda
1½ cups sugar	1 teaspoon salt
½ cup cocoa	1 teaspoon vanilla
½ cup shortening	3 eggs
1 cup milk	

Heat oven to 350°. Grease and flour 2 round pans, 8 × 1½ inches. Beat all ingredients in large bowl on medium speed, scraping bowl constantly, until blended, 30 seconds. Beat on high speed, scraping bowl occasionally, 3 minutes. Pour into pans.

Bake until wooden pick inserted in center comes out clean, 35 to 40 minutes. Cool 10 minutes; remove from pans. Cool completely.

Chocolate-Peanut Butter Frosting

3 cups powdered sugar	⅓ cup peanut butter
3 tablespoons cocoa	⅓ cup milk

Beat all ingredients on medium speed until smooth and spreading consistency. If necessary, stir in additional milk, ½ teaspoon at a time.

○ *Time-saver Tip:* Substitute 1 package (18.5 ounces) chocolate fudge cake mix with pudding for the Chocolate Fudge Cake. Prepare and bake as directed on package.

Zoo Cake

Banana-Nut Cake (below)   *Animal crackers*
Creamy Cocoa Frosting   *Assorted small gumdrops*
   (below)

Bake Banana-Nut Cake as directed. Place cake on large tray or aluminum foil-covered cardboard, about 14 × 10 inches. Frost sides and top of cake with Creamy Cocoa Frosting (frosting on top should be ¼ inch thick).

Place animal crackers about 1 inch apart around top edge of cake, pressing gently into frosting to hold upright. Place gumdrops between each cracker. Place the number of candles appropriate to the child's birthday in an equal number of gumdrops. Arrange on cake. 12 to 15 servings.

Banana-Nut Cake

2⅓ cups all-purpose flour	1¼ teaspoons baking
1⅔ cups sugar	powder
⅔ cup shortening	1¼ teaspoons baking soda
1¼ cups mashed bananas	1 teaspoon salt
(about 3 medium)	3 eggs
⅔ cup buttermilk	⅔ cup finely chopped
	nuts

Heat oven to 350°. Grease and flour rectangular pan, 13 × 9 × 2 inches. Beat all ingredients in large bowl on medium speed, scraping bowl constantly, until blended, about 30 seconds. Beat on high speed, scraping bowl occasionally, 3 minutes. Pour into pan.

Bake until wooden pick inserted in center comes out clean, 45 to 50 minutes. Cool 10 minutes; remove from pan. Cool completely.

Creamy Cocoa Frosting

3 cups powdered sugar	1½ teaspoons vanilla
⅓ cup cocoa	3 tablespoons milk
⅓ cup margarine or	
butter, softened	

Beat all ingredients on medium speed until smooth and spreading consistency. If necessary, stir in additional milk, ½ teaspoon at a time.

○ *Time-saver Tip:* Substitute 1 package (18.5 ounces) banana, yellow or devils food cake mix with pudding for the Banana-Nut Cake. Prepare and bake as directed on package. Substitute 1 tub (16.5 ounces) chocolate ready-to-spread frosting for the Creamy Cocoa Frosting.

Clockwise from top: Zoo Cake, Corral Cake (page 77), Train Birthday Cake (page 77)

Bunny Cake

Carrot Cake (below)
Pineapple Frosting (below)
Red food color
Large marshmallow

Large black gumdrop
Small pink gumdrop
Shoestring licorice
Small colored candies

Bake Carrot Cake as directed. Cut one cake layer as shown in diagram. Arrange pieces on large tray or aluminum foil-covered cardboard, 18 × 15 inches. Reserve ¾ cup Pineapple Frosting. Frost head and ears with remaining frosting, leaving narrow portion in center of ears unfrosted. Tint reserved frosting pink with 1 or 2 drops red food color. Frost tie and center of ears with pink frosting.

Cut marshmallow horizontally into halves; press halves into frosting for eyes. Add thin slices of black gumdrop for pupils of eyes and pink gumdrop for nose. Add short strips of shoestring licorice for eyelashes. Outline mouth with shoestring licorice or with wooden pick dipped into food color. Place candies on tie. 14 to 16 servings.

Carrot Cake

2 cups all-purpose flour	1 teaspoon salt
2 cups finely shredded carrots (about 4 medium)	1 teaspoon ground cinnamon
1¼ cups sugar	1 teaspoon ground cloves
½ cup vegetable oil	1 teaspoon ground nutmeg
⅓ cup water	1 teaspoon vanilla
1¼ teaspoons baking soda	3 eggs
	1 cup chopped nuts

Heat oven to 350°. Grease and flour 2 round pans, 8 or 9 × 1½ inches. Beat all ingredients in large bowl on medium speed, scraping bowl constantly, until blended, about 1 minute. Beat on medium speed, scraping bowl occasionally, 2 minutes. Pour into pans.

Bake until wooden pick inserted in center comes out clean, 35 to 40 minutes. Cool 10 minutes; remove from pans. Cool completely.

Pineapple Frosting

½ cup sugar	1 teaspoon finely shredded lemon peel
¼ cup light corn syrup	
2 tablespoons water	1 can (about 8¼ ounces) crushed pineapple, well drained
2 egg whites	

Mix sugar, corn syrup and water in saucepan. Cover and heat to rolling boil over medium heat.

Uncover and boil rapidly until candy thermometer registers 242° or until small amount of mixture dropped into very cold water forms a firm ball that holds its shape until pressed.

As mixture boils, beat egg whites until stiff peaks form. Pour hot syrup very slowly in a thin stream into egg whites, beating constantly on medium speed. Beat on high speed until stiff peaks form. Stir in lemon peel and pineapple.

○ *Time-saver Tip:* Substitute 1 package (18.5 ounces) yellow cake mix with pudding for the Carrot Cake. Prepare and bake as directed on package. Substitute 1 package (7.2 ounces) fluffy white frosting mix for the Pineapple Frosting. Prepare as directed on package except after beating, fold in 1 teaspoon finely shredded lemon peel and 1 can (8¼ ounces) crushed pineapple, well drained.

Cutting and Assembling Bunny Cake

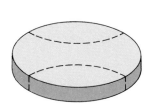

Cut 1 layer to form ears and bow.

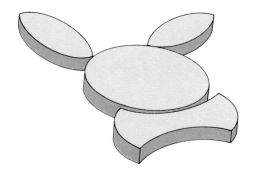

Arrange pieces of bunny on tray (turn one ear to side if desired.)

Bunny Cake

Car Cake

Brown Sugar Fudge Cake (below)
Penuche Frosting (right)
Black shoestring licorice
Small colored candies
2 peppermint candies or large gumdrops

Bake Brown Sugar Fudge Cake as directed. Cut cake as shown in diagram. Freeze cut pieces uncovered about 1 hour for easier frosting if desired. Arrange pieces to form car on large tray or aluminum foil-covered cardboard, about 15 × 12 inches. If necessary, trim wheels to join evenly.

Mix ⅓ cup of the Penuche Frosting and ½ to 1 teaspoon milk to make a thinner consistency; use to seal in crumbs on cut edges and to join pieces. Frost sides and top of cake with remaining frosting.

Use shoestring licorice for windows, door, fenders and wheels. Outline running board, trunk and top of car with candies. Use peppermint candies for hubs of wheels. 14 to 16 servings.

Brown Sugar Fudge Cake

2 cups all-purpose flour
2 cups packed brown sugar
½ cup shortening
1 cup buttermilk
1 teaspoon baking soda
¾ teaspoon salt
1 teaspoon vanilla
3 eggs
2 ounces melted unsweetened chocolate (cool)

Heat oven to 350°. Grease and flour rectangular pan, 13 × 9 × 2 inches. Beat all ingredients in large bowl on medium speed, scraping bowl constantly, until blended, about 30 seconds. Beat on high speed, scraping bowl occasionally, 3 minutes. Pour into pan.

Bake until wooden pick inserted in center comes out clean, 40 to 45 minutes. Cool 10 minutes; remove from pan. Cool completely.

Penuche Frosting

½ cup margarine or butter
1 cup packed brown sugar
¼ cup milk
2 cups powdered sugar

Heat margarine in 2-quart saucepan until melted. Stir in brown sugar. Heat to boiling, stirring constantly. Boil and stir over low heat 2 minutes. Stir in milk; heat to boiling. Remove from heat and cool to lukewarm. Stir in powdered sugar gradually. Place pan of frosting in bowl of cold water; beat until frosting is smooth and spreading consistency. If frosting becomes too stiff, stir in additional milk, 1 teaspoon at a time.

○ Time-saver Tip: Substitute 1 package (18.5 ounces) chocolate fudge cake mix with pudding for the Brown Sugar Fudge Cake. Prepare and bake as directed on package.

Cutting and Assembling Car Cake

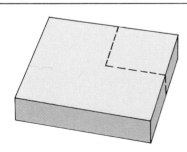 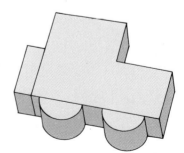

Cut 4 × 5-inch piece from one end of cake.

Cut piece into 4-inch circle and 1-inch strip; cut circle into half.

Arrange pieces to form trunk and wheels of car.

Guitar Cake

Caramel Chocolate Chip
Cake (below)
Satiny Beige Frosting
(below)

Black or red shoestring
licorice
Colored sugar
Assorted candies
4 small lollipops

Bake Caramel Chocolate Chip Cake as directed.
Cut cake as shown in diagram. Arrange cake pieces
on large tray or aluminum foil-covered cardboard,
about 20 × 12 inches, to form guitar. (Use remaining
pieces as desired.)

Frost cake with Satiny Beige Frosting, joining pieces
together. Use shoestring licorice to form sound
hole. Sprinkle colored sugar in rectangle, 3½ × 1
inch, below sound hole for string bar.

Use short piece of shoestring licorice to make cross-
pieces on neck for fretted fingerboard. Place longer shoestring licorice from string bar to top of neck
for the strings. Place candies around edge of guitar,
on the string bar and at the top of the neck. Insert 2
small lollipops in each triangular piece at top of
tuning pegs. 14 to 16 servings.

Caramel Chocolate Chip Cake

2 cups all-purpose flour
1 cup packed brown
   sugar
½ cup granulated sugar
½ cup shortening
1¼ cups milk
3 teaspoons baking
   powder
1 teaspoon salt

½ teaspoon baking soda
1½ teaspoons vanilla
3 eggs
½ cup semisweet
   chocolate chips,
   finely chopped, or
½ cup miniature
   chocolate chips

Heat oven to 350°. Grease and flour rectangular
pan, 13 × 9 × 2 inches. Beat all ingredients in large
bowl on medium speed, scraping bowl constantly,
until blended, about 30 seconds. Beat on high
speed, scraping bowl occasionally, 3 minutes. Pour
into pan.

Bake until wooden pick inserted in center comes
out clean, 40 to 45 minutes. Cool 10 minutes; remove from pan. Cool completely.

Satiny Beige Frosting

½ cup packed brown
   sugar
¼ cup light corn syrup

2 tablespoons water
2 egg whites
½ teaspoon vanilla

Mix brown sugar, corn syrup and water in 1-quart
saucepan. Cover and heat to rolling boil over

medium heat. Uncover and boil rapidly until candy
thermometer registers 242° or until small amount
of mixture dropped into very cold water forms a
firm ball that holds its shape until pressed.

As mixture boils, beat egg whites in small bowl just
until stiff peaks form. Pour hot syrup very slowly in
a thin stream into egg whites, beating constantly on
medium speed. Add vanilla; beat on high speed
until stiff peaks form.

○ *Time-saver Tip:* Substitute 1 package (18.5
ounces) yellow cake mix with pudding for the
Caramel Chocolate Chip Cake. Prepare and bake
as directed on package. Substitute 1 package (7.2
ounces) fluffy white frosting mix for the Satiny
Beige Frosting. Prepare as directed on package.

Cutting and Assembling Guitar Cake

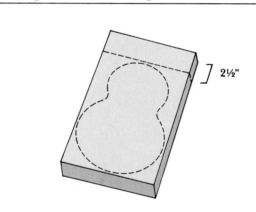

2½"

Carefully cut cake into 2 pieces.

Arrange cake pieces to form guitar.

Panda Cake

Oatmeal-Spice Cake (right)
White Mountain Frosting (page 16)
½ cup flaked coconut
8 chocolate wafers, about 2 inches in diameter
1 large marshmallow
2 chocolate-covered candies
1 small black or red gumdrop
Black shoestring licorice
⅓ cup flaked coconut
1 teaspoon cocoa

Bake Oatmeal-Spice Cake as directed. Cut small piece from one side of 9-inch layer as shown in diagram. Place 9-inch layer on large tray or aluminum foil-covered cardboard, about 16 × 10 inches. Join 8-inch layer to cut section for head of panda.

Frost cake with White Mountain Frosting. Cover top ¾ portion of body of panda with ½ cup flaked coconut. Press 2 wafers into top of head at 45° angle for ears. Place 2 wafers for background of eyes and 4 on body for paws, placing bottom 2 wafers at 45° angle on bottom edge of cake.

Cut marshmallow crosswise into halves; place each half on a chocolate wafer for eyes. Place chocolate candies on marshmallow halves for pupils; fasten with small dab of frosting if necessary. Use small gumdrop for nose and shoestring licorice for mouth and outline of legs. Toss ⅓ cup coconut and the cocoa; carefully sprinkle within outline of legs and on bottom portion of body. 14 to 16 servings.

Oatmeal-Spice Cake

1½ cups all-purpose flour
1 cup quick-cooking oats
1 cup packed brown sugar
½ cup granulated sugar
½ cup shortening
1 cup water
1½ teaspoons baking soda
1 teaspoon ground cinnamon
½ teaspoon salt
½ teaspoon ground nutmeg, if desired
2 tablespoons molasses
2 eggs

Heat oven to 350°. Grease and flour round pan, 8 × 1½ inches, and round pan, 9 × 1½ inches. Beat all ingredients in large bowl on medium speed, scraping bowl constantly, until blended, about 30 seconds. Beat on high speed, scraping bowl occasionally, 3 minutes. Pour into pans. (Batter in pans should be the same level—measure depth of batter with a wooden pick.)

Bake until wooden pick inserted in center comes out clean, 30 to 35 minutes. Cool 10 minutes; remove from pans. Cool completely.

○ *Time-saver Tip:* Substitute 1 package (18.5 ounces) spice, yellow or devils food cake mix with pudding for the Oatmeal-Spice Cake. Prepare and bake as directed on package. Substitute 1 package (7.2 ounces) fluffy white frosting mix for the White Mountain Frosting. Prepare as directed on the package.

Cutting and Assembling Panda Cake

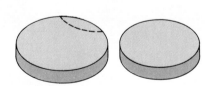

Cut small piece from one side of 9-inch layer.

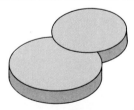

Join 8-inch layer to cut section of 9-inch layer.

Sailboat Cake

*Buttermilk Spice Cake
(below)*
*White Mountain
Frosting (page 16)*
1 tablespoon cocoa

*14 × 4-inch piece of
aluminum foil**
*Ring-shaped hard candy
mints*

Bake Buttermilk Spice Cake as directed. Cut cake as shown in diagram. Arrange pieces to form sailboat on large tray or aluminum foil-covered cardboard, about 20 × 18 inches, leaving space between sails for mast. Reserve 1 cup White Mountain Frosting; frost sails with remaining frosting.

Sift cocoa over reserved frosting; gently fold in cocoa until blended. Frost hull of sailboat with cocoa frosting. Roll up aluminum foil for mast; place between sails. Use candy mints for portholes or decorate as desired. 14 to 16 servings.

*A 14 × 4-inch piece of wrapping or shelf paper can be substituted for aluminum foil; secure with tape.

Buttermilk Spice Cake

*2½ cups all-purpose flour
or cake flour*
1 cup granulated sugar
*¾ cup packed brown
sugar*
½ cup shortening
1⅓ cups buttermilk
*1 teaspoon baking
powder*
1 teaspoon baking soda

1 teaspoon salt
*¾ teaspoon ground
cinnamon*
*¾ teaspoon ground
allspice*
½ teaspoon ground cloves
*½ teaspoon ground
nutmeg*
3 eggs

Heat oven to 350°. Grease and flour rectangular pan, 13 × 9 × 2 inches. Beat all ingredients in large bowl on medium speed, scraping bowl constantly, until blended, about 30 seconds. Beat on high speed, scraping bowl occasionally, 3 minutes. Pour into pan.

Bake until wooden pick inserted in center comes out clean, 40 to 45 minutes. Cool 10 minutes; remove from pan. Cool completely.

○ *Time-saver Tip:* Substitute 1 package (18.5 ounces) spice, devils food or yellow cake mix with pudding for the Buttermilk Spice Cake. Prepare and bake as directed on package. Substitute 1 package (7.2 ounces) fluffy white frosting mix for the White Mountain Frosting. Prepare as directed on the package.

Cutting and Assembling Sailboat Cake

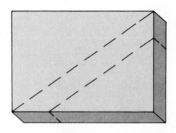

Cut cake diagonally into 3 pieces.

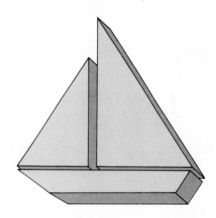

Arrange pieces to form sailboat, leaving space between sails for mast.

BACKGROUNDS FOR CUT-UP CAKES

If you do not have a tray large enough for a cut-up cake, use a large piece of cardboard cut to the correct size, a large breadboard or an inverted jelly roll pan and cover with aluminum or colored foil. To vary the color or fit the occasion, use other paper, such as shelf paper, gift wrap or colored tissue paper, then cover with plastic wrap. If you wish, messages or other designs can be added to the background around the cake. Use a marking pencil to write on foil or plastic wrap.

Graduation Cake

This cake can be decorated in the graduate's school colors. If red is one of the colors used, paste food color is recommended for a more vivid shade.

Chocolate-Pecan Cake (right)
Vanilla Butter Frosting (right)
Yellow, green and blue food color

Bake Chocolate-Pecan Cake as directed. Repeat for second cake. Place cakes topside up and together lengthwise on large tray, mirror or aluminum foil-covered cardboard, about 20 × 15 inches. (Trim long sides of each cake to resemble open book if desired.) Reserve 1¼ cups Vanilla Butter Frosting for decorating. Tint 1 cup of the remaining frosting yellow with 3 drops yellow food color.

Frost sides of cakes with yellow frosting. Draw decorating comb horizontally through frosting on all sides to resemble pages of a book. Frost tops of cakes with remaining frosting to resemble open pages of a book.

Tint ¾ cup of the reserved frosting blue with 5 or 6 drops blue food color. Tint remaining ½ cup frosting green with 2 or 3 drops green food color. Place green frosting in decorating bag with writing tip #2; pipe stems for spray of flowers.

Make desired number of drop flowers with blue frosting and drop flower tip #177 (see page 8). Write desired message and make bead border around base and along top center of cake with writing tip #2 (see page 9). Make leaves with green frosting and leaf tip #352. Pipe dots on flowers with yellow frosting and writing tip #2. If desired,

add miniature diploma. Roll up piece of paper, 6 × 5 inches; tie blue and yellow ribbons around center and place on cake. 30 servings, 3 × 2½ inches.

Chocolate-Pecan Cake

1⅔ cups all-purpose flour	1¼ teaspoons baking soda
1½ cups sugar	1 teaspoon salt
½ cup cocoa	1 teaspoon vanilla
½ cup shortening	3 eggs
1 cup milk	½ cup chopped pecans

Heat oven to 350°. Grease and flour rectangular pan, 13 × 9 × 2 inches. Beat all ingredients in large bowl on medium speed, scraping bowl constantly, until blended, about 30 seconds. Beat on high speed, scraping bowl occasionally, 3 minutes. Pour into pan.

Bake until wooden pick inserted in center comes out clean, 35 to 40 minutes. Cool 10 minutes; remove from pan. Cool completely. 15 servings.

Vanilla Butter Frosting

9 cups powdered sugar	2 teaspoons vanilla
½ cup margarine or butter, softened	⅓ cup plus 1 tablespoon milk
½ cup shortening	

Beat all ingredients on medium speed until smooth and spreading consistency. If necessary, stir in additional milk, 1 teaspoon at a time.

○ *Time-saver Tip:* Substitute 2 packages (18.5 ounces each) devils food or chocolate fudge cake mix with pudding for the Chocolate-Pecan Cakes. Prepare and bake as directed on package except stir ½ cup chopped pecans into each batter.

FRESH FLOWER DECORATIONS

Fresh flowers can enhance the attractiveness of a cake. To use them, select those which can last out of water for several hours without wilting. Appropriate choices are daisies, chrysanthemums and buttercups. Consult your local florist for other suggestions. If the flowers may have been sprayed with a pesticide, dip them in soapy water, rinse and dry before placing them on the cake. A small piece of plastic wrap also can be placed beneath the portion of the flower that will touch the cake. Arrange greenery such as ferns around the base.

Celebration Squares

These versatile cake squares can be adapted to celebrate any occasion. Prepare them for a house-warming or bon voyage party, a promotion, a birthday, to say Happy New Year or just Good Luck.

Yellow Cake (below)
Glaze (below)
2 cups powdered sugar

Few drops food color
2 to 3 tablespoons water

Bake Yellow Cake as directed. Cut cake into 2-inch squares. Place one at a time on wire rack over large bowl. Pour Glaze over squares to cover top and sides. (Glaze can be reheated and used again.)

Mix powdered sugar, desired food color and water—just enough to make a frosting that can be used easily in a decorating bag or envelope cone. Place in decorating bag with writing tip #3. Write one of the letters of desired message on each of the required number of squares. Arrange squares on large tray or aluminum foil-covered cardboard to spell out greeting. Write names of guests on remaining squares if desired. About 35 squares.

Yellow Cake

1¾ cups sugar
⅔ cup margarine or
   butter, softened
1½ teaspoons vanilla
2 eggs

2¾ cups all-purpose flour
2½ teaspoons baking
   powder
1 teaspoon salt
1¼ cups milk

Heat oven to 350°. Grease and flour jelly roll pan, 15½ × 10½ × 1 inch. Beat sugar, margarine, vanilla and eggs in large bowl on medium speed, scraping bowl constantly, until blended, about 30 seconds. Beat on high speed, scraping bowl occasionally, 5 minutes. Beat in flour, baking powder and salt alternately with milk on low speed. Pour into pan.

Bake until wooden pick inserted in center comes out clean, 25 to 30 minutes. Cool completely.

Glaze

8 cups powdered sugar
½ cup water
½ cup light corn syrup

1½ teaspoons almond
   extract

Beat all ingredients in top of double boiler until smooth. Heat just until lukewarm; remove from heat. Let glaze remain over hot water to prevent thickening. If necessary, add hot water, a few drops at a time, for desired consistency.

"King for a Day" Cake

The message can read "Queen for a Day." This is the perfect cake to celebrate a birthday, a promotion or any special achievement.

Chocolate Spice Cake
   (below)
White Mountain Frosting
   (page 16)

Chocolate Decorator
   Frosting (below)
Sliced gumdrops or small
   colored candies

Bake Chocolate Spice Cake as directed. Fill layers and frost cake with White Mountain Frosting, making top smooth. Place Chocolate Decorator Frosting in decorating bag with writing tip #5. Outline a crown on top of cake; write a name below. Place gumdrop slices at points of crown. 12 to 16 servings.

Chocolate Spice Cake

2 cups all-purpose
   flour or cake flour
2 cups sugar
½ cup shortening
¾ cup water
¾ cup buttermilk
2 teaspoons ground
   cinnamon
1 teaspoon baking soda

1 teaspoon salt
½ teaspoon baking
   powder
½ teaspoon ground
   nutmeg
4 ounces melted
   unsweetened
   chocolate (cool)
2 eggs

Heat oven to 350°. Grease and flour 2 round pans, 9 × 1½ inches, or 3 round pans, 8 × 1½ inches. Beat all ingredients in large bowl on medium speed, scraping bowl constantly, until blended, about 30 seconds. Beat on high speed, scraping bowl occasionally, 3 minutes. Pour into pans.

Bake until wooden pick inserted in center comes out clean, 30 to 35 minutes. Cool 10 minutes; remove from pans. Cool completely.

Chocolate Decorator Frosting

Mix ½ cup powdered sugar, 2 teaspoons cocoa and 1½ to 2 teaspoons water until smooth and desired consistency.

○ Time-saver Tip: Substitute 1 package (18.5 ounces) devils food cake mix with pudding for the Chocolate Spice Cake. Prepare and bake as directed on package for 9-inch rounds except add 2 teaspoons ground cinnamon and ½ teaspoon ground nutmeg before beating. Substitute 1 package (7.2 ounces) fluffy white frosting mix for the White Mountain Frosting. Prepare as directed on the package.

"King for a Day" Cake, center, Celebration Squares, top and bottom

Housewarming Cake

With creative free-hand drawing you can adapt this cake to many occasions. Consider personalizing it as a birthday cake by picturing hobbies of the honored guest.

Whole Wheat Applesauce Cake (below)	¼ cup cocoa
	Green, yellow and red
Vanilla Butter Frosting (right)	food color

Bake Whole Wheat Applesauce Cake as directed. Reserve 1¼ cups Vanilla Butter Frosting for decorating. Frost cake with remaining frosting, making top smooth. Make design on sides with decorating comb if desired.

Sift ¼ cup cocoa over ⅔ cup of the reserved frosting; stir until smooth. Stir 3 or 4 drops green food color into ⅓ cup of the reserved frosting. Stir 6 drops yellow and 1 drop red food color into remaining frosting. Keep frostings covered to prevent drying.

Place cocoa frosting in decorating bag with writing tip #2. Outline houses, path, fence, tree trunk and write message. Pipe border around top edge of cake with same frosting and star tip #18.

Outline flowers and sun with orange frosting and writing tip #2. Fill in trees and bushes with green frosting and star tip #18. Outline stems and leaves for flowers with same frosting and writing tip #2.

Whole Wheat Applesauce Cake

1¼ cups all-purpose flour	¾ teaspoon ground
1¼ cups whole wheat flour	cinnamon
1⅔ cups sugar	½ teaspoon ground cloves
½ cup shortening	½ teaspoon ground allspice
1½ cups canned applesauce	¼ teaspoon baking powder
½ cup water	2 eggs
1½ teaspoons baking soda	1 cup raisins
1½ teaspoons salt	½ cup chopped walnuts

Heat oven to 350°. Grease and flour rectangular pan, 13×9×2 inches. Beat all ingredients in large bowl on medium speed, scraping bowl constantly, until blended, about 30 seconds. Beat on high speed, scraping bowl occasionally, 3 minutes. Pour into pan.

Bake until wooden pick inserted in center comes out clean, 60 to 65 minutes. Cool 10 minutes; remove from pan if desired. Cool completely.

Vanilla Butter Frosting

5 cups powdered sugar	2 teaspoons vanilla
½ cup margarine or butter, softened	¼ cup milk

Beat all ingredients on medium speed until smooth and spreading consistency. If necessary, stir in additional milk, 1 teaspoon at a time.

○ *Time-saver Tip:* Substitute 1 package (18.5 ounces) devils food, yellow or spice cake mix with pudding for the Whole Wheat Applesauce Cake. Prepare and bake as directed on package.

SHORTENING IN CAKES

When our recipes call for margarine or butter, they have been tested using stick-type margarine and butter. We think this brings out the flavor of the other ingredients.

Unsalted butter, now available, is butter to which no salt has been added. Recipes that specify unsalted butter are usually adaptations of European recipes as most European butter is unsalted.

If you care to experiment with substituting unsalted butter for the margarine or butter, be sure to keep the proportion of shortening to margarine or butter the same.

And unless oil is called for, as with chiffon-type cakes, never substitute oil for shortening, margarine or butter, even if the recipe calls for melted shortening.

Special Cakes

Triple Chocolate Cake

Chocolate Angel Food Cake (below)
Chocolate Fluff (below)

Chocolate Triangles (below) or dark chocolate-covered thin mints

Bake Chocolate Angel Food Cake as directed. Remove cake from pan. Split cake to make 3 layers (see page 13). Fill each layer with 1 cup Chocolate Fluff; frost cake with remaining frosting. Decorate with chocolate triangles. Refrigerate any remaining cake. 12 to 16 servings.

Chocolate Angel Food Cake

1½ cups powdered sugar
¾ cup cake flour
¼ cup cocoa
1½ cups egg whites (about 12)

1½ teaspoons cream of tartar
1 cup granulated sugar
¼ teaspoon salt
1½ teaspoons vanilla

Heat oven to 375°. Mix powdered sugar, flour and cocoa. Beat egg whites and cream of tartar in large bowl on medium speed until foamy. Beat in granulated sugar on high speed, 2 tablespoons at a time; continue beating until stiff and glossy. Add salt and vanilla with the last addition of sugar. Do not underbeat.

Sprinkle flour mixture, ¼ cup at a time, over meringue, folding in just until flour mixture disappears. Push batter into ungreased tube pan, 10 × 4 inches. Cut gently through the batter with a metal spatula.

Bake until cracks feel dry and top springs back when touched lightly, 30 to 35 minutes. Invert pan on heatproof funnel; let hang until cake is cold.

Chocolate Fluff

3 cups chilled whipping cream
1½ cups powdered sugar

¾ cup cocoa
¼ teaspoon salt

Beat all ingredients in chilled bowl until stiff.

Chocolate Triangles

Heat 1 bar (4 ounces) sweet cooking chocolate over low heat until melted. Spread over outside bottom of square pan, 8 × 8 × 2 inches. Refrigerate until firm; bring to room temperature. Cut into squares; cut squares diagonally into halves for triangles. Refrigerate until ready to use.

Pink Coconut Cake

Coconut Angel Food Cake (below)

White Mountain Frosting (page 16)
Pink Coconut (below)

Bake Coconut Angel Food Cake as directed. Remove cake from pan. Frost with White Mountain Frosting. Mark top and side into 8 equal wedges and panels. Sprinkle Pink Coconut over alternate wedges; press onto alternate side panels. Press narrow strip of coconut across tops and down sides of white panels if desired. 12 to 16 servings.

Coconut Angel Food Cake

1½ cups powdered sugar
1 cup cake flour
1½ cups egg whites (about 12)
1½ teaspoons cream of tartar

1 cup granulated sugar
¼ teaspoon salt
1½ teaspoons vanilla
½ teaspoon almond extract
1 cup flaked coconut

Heat oven to 375°. Mix powdered sugar and flour. Beat egg whites and cream of tartar in large bowl on medium speed until foamy. Beat in granulated sugar on high speed, 2 tablespoons at a time; continue beating until stiff and glossy. Add salt, vanilla and almond extract with the last addition of sugar. Do not underbeat.

Sprinkle flour-sugar mixture, ¼ cup at a time, over meringue, folding in just until flour-sugar mixture disappears. Fold in flaked coconut, ½ cup at a time. Push batter into ungreased tube pan, 10 × 4 inches. Cut gently through batter with metal spatula.

Bake until cracks feel dry and top springs back when touched lightly, 35 to 40 minutes. Invert pan on heatproof funnel; let hang until cake is cold.

Pink Coconut

Shake 1½ cups flaked coconut and 2 drops red food color in tightly covered jar until coconut is evenly tinted.

○ *Time-saver Tip:* Substitute 1 package (16 ounces) white angel food cake mix for the Coconut Angel Food Cake. Prepare and bake as directed on package except fold 1 cup flaked coconut into batter, ½ cup at a time. Substitute 1 package (7.2 ounces) fluffy white frosting mix for the White Mountain Frosting. Prepare as directed on package.

Pink Coconut Cake, top, Triple Chocolate Cake, bottom

Pictured on preceding page: Clockwise from left: Deluxe Chocolate Cake (page 119), Apricot-glazed Pound Cake (page 139), Rhubarb-Butterscotch Meringue Cake (page 148)

Chocolate Alexander Cake

Brown Sugar Angel
Food Cake (below)
½ cup white crème de
cacao
2 tablespoons whipping
cream

1½ cups chilled
whipping cream
⅓ cup powdered sugar
¼ cup white crème de
cacao
Chocolate Curls
(page 119)

Bake Brown Sugar Angel Food Cake as directed. Remove cake from pan; place on serving plate. Make holes of various depths in cake with 5-inch skewer. Mix ½ cup crème de cacao and 2 tablespoons whipping cream; pour into holes.

Beat 1½ cups whipping cream and the powdered sugar in chilled bowl until stiff peaks form; fold in ¼ cup crème de cacao. Frost cake. Coat top of cake with Chocolate Curls. Refrigerate any remaining cake. 12 to 16 servings.

Brown Sugar Angel Food Cake

1¼ cups packed brown
sugar
1 cup cake flour
1½ cups egg whites
(about 12)
1½ teaspoons cream of
tartar

¾ cup packed brown
sugar
¼ teaspoon salt
1½ teaspoons vanilla
½ teaspoon almond
extract

Heat oven to 375°. Beat 1¼ cups brown sugar and the flour with hand beater until no longer lumpy (break up any remaining lumps with fingers). Beat egg whites and cream of tartar in large bowl on medium speed until foamy. Beat in ¾ cup brown sugar on high speed, 2 tablespoons at a time; continue beating until stiff and glossy. Add salt, vanilla and almond extract with the last addition of sugar. Do not underbeat.

Sprinkle flour-sugar mixture, ¼ cup at a time, over meringue, folding in just until flour-sugar mixture disappears. Push batter into ungreased tube pan, 10 × 4 inches. Cut gently through the batter with a metal spatula.

Bake until cracks feel dry and top springs back when touched lightly, 30 to 35 minutes. Invert pan on heatproof funnel; let hang until cake is cold.

Caramel Fluff Cake

Custard Angel Food Cake
(below)

Caramel Fluff (below)
Chocolate Leaves
(page 57)

Bake Custard Angel Food Cake as directed. Remove cake from pan. Frost with Caramel Fluff. Decorate with a garland of Chocolate Leaves. Refrigerate any remaining cake. 12 to 16 servings.

Custard Angel Food Cake

⅓ cup milk, scalded
3 egg yolks, slightly
beaten
1 cup cake flour
¾ cup plus 2 tablespoons
sugar
½ teaspoon ground
nutmeg

1½ cups egg whites
(about 12)
1½ teaspoons cream of
tartar
¾ cup sugar
¼ teaspoon salt
2½ teaspoons vanilla

Heat oven to 375°. Stir hot milk into egg yolks; cover and cool. Mix flour, ¾ cup plus 2 tablespoons sugar and the nutmeg. Beat egg whites and cream of tartar in large bowl on medium speed until foamy. Beat in ¾ cup sugar on high speed, 2 tablespoons at a time; continue beating until stiff and glossy. Add salt and vanilla with the last addition of sugar. Do not underbeat.

Sprinkle flour-sugar mixture, ¼ cup at a time, over meringue, folding in just until flour-sugar mixture disappears. Fold 1½ cups angel food batter into cooled custard mixture; fold custard mixture, about ⅓ at a time, into angel food batter just until no yellow streaks remain. Push batter into ungreased tube pan, 10 × 4 inches. Cut gently through the batter with a metal spatula.

Bake until cracks feel dry and top springs back when touched lightly, 30 to 35 minutes. Invert pan on heatproof funnel; let hang until cake is cold.

Caramel Fluff

Beat 2 cups chilled whipping cream, ¾ cup packed brown sugar and 1 teaspoon vanilla in chilled bowl until stiff.

Caramel Fluff Cake, top, Chocolate Alexander Cake, bottom,

Peppermint Whipped Cream Cake

Peppermint Whipped Cream Cake

Angel Food Cake
Supreme (right)
Peppermint Whipped
Cream (right)

3 tablespoons crushed
    peppermint candy

Bake Angel Food Cake Supreme as directed. Remove cake from pan; place upside down. Slice off top of cake about 1 inch down (see page 13) and reserve. Cut down into cake 1 inch from outer edge and 1 inch from edge of hole, leaving substantial "walls" on each side. Remove center with a spoon or curved knife, being careful to leave a base of cake 1 inch thick.

Spoon half the Peppermint Whipped Cream into cake cavity. Press mixture firmly into cavity.

Replace top of cake and press gently. Frost cake with remaining whipped cream. Refrigerate at least 4 hours. Just before serving, sprinkle with crushed candy. Refrigerate any remaining cake. 12 to 16 servings.

Angel Food Cake Supreme

  1 cup cake flour
 ³⁄₄ cup plus 2
      tablespoons sugar
1¹⁄₂ cups egg whites
      (about 12)
1¹⁄₂ teaspoons cream of
      tartar

 ³⁄₄ cup sugar
 ¹⁄₄ teaspoon salt
  1 teaspoon peppermint
      extract
      Red food color

Heat oven to 375°. Mix flour and ¾ cup plus 2 tablespoons sugar. Beat egg whites and cream of tartar in large bowl on medium speed until foamy. Beat in ¾ cup sugar on high speed, 2 tablespoons at a time; continue beating until stiff and glossy. Add salt and peppermint extract with the last addition of sugar. Do not underbeat.

Sprinkle flour-sugar mixture, ¼ cup at a time, over meringue, folding in just until flour-sugar mixture disappears. Sprinkle few drops food color over batter; fold in with 3 or 4 strokes to streak through batter. Push batter into ungreased tube pan, 10 × 4 inches. Cut gently through batter with spatula.

Bake until cracks feel dry and top springs back when touched lightly, 30 to 35 minutes. Invert pan on heatproof funnel; let hang until cake is cold.

Peppermint Whipped Cream

2 cups chilled whipping
    cream
1 cup powdered sugar

1 teaspoon peppermint
    extract
8 drops red food color

Beat all ingredients in chilled bowl until stiff.

○ *Time-saver Tip:* Substitute 1 package (16 ounces) white angel food cake mix for the Angel Food Cake Supreme. Prepare and bake as directed on package.

WHIPPED CREAM ROSETTES

Cream can be whipped and stored in refrigerator up to 2 hours before using. For longer storage or to use leftover whipped cream, make rosettes (see page 8) and place on aluminum foil; freeze. When frozen solid, wrap and store in freezer. Use for instant toppings on cakes or other desserts.

Daffodil Cake

*Marbled Custard Angel
Food Cake (below)*

*Lemon Fluff (below)
Lemon Flowers (right)*

Bake Marbled Custard Angel Food Cake as directed. Remove cake from pan. Frost with Lemon Fluff. Decorate with Lemon Flowers. 12 to 16 servings.

Marbled Custard Angel Food Cake

1½ cups powdered sugar
  1 cup cake flour
1½ cups egg whites
    (about 12)
1½ teaspoons cream of
    tartar

1 cup granulated
    sugar
¼ teaspoon salt
1 teaspoon vanilla
4 egg yolks
1 teaspoon lemon extract

Heat oven to 375°. Mix powdered sugar and flour. Beat egg whites and cream of tartar in large bowl on medium speed until foamy. Beat in granulated sugar on high speed, 2 tablespoons at a time; continue beating until stiff and glossy. Add salt and vanilla with the last addition of sugar. Do not underbeat. Beat egg yolks and lemon extract until very thick and lemon colored, about 5 minutes.

Sprinkle flour-sugar mixture, ¼ cup at a time, over meringue, folding in just until flour-sugar mixture disappears. Pour half of the batter into another bowl; fold in egg yolk mixture. Spoon yellow and white batters alternately into ungreased tube pan, 10 × 4 inches. Cut gently through batters to swirl.

Bake until cracks feel dry and top springs back when touched lightly, 30 to 35 minutes. Invert pan on heatproof funnel; let hang until cake is cold.

Lemon Fluff

½ cup sugar
¼ cup light corn syrup
2 tablespoons water
2 egg whites
¼ teaspoon finely
    shredded lemon peel

1 tablespoon lemon
    juice
10 drops yellow food
    color

Mix sugar, corn syrup and water in 1-quart saucepan. Cover and heat to rolling boil over medium heat. Uncover and boil rapidly until candy thermometer registers 242° or until small amount of mixture dropped into very cold water forms a firm ball that holds its shape until pressed.

As mixture boils, beat egg whites in small bowl just until stiff peaks form. Pour hot syrup very slowly in a thin stream into egg whites, beating constantly on

Daffodil Cake

medium speed. Beat on high speed until stiff peaks form. Beat in lemon peel, lemon juice and the food color.

Lemon Flowers

Cut 6 to 8 lemon candy slices into 5 wedges each for petals. Cut "peel" from lime candy slices for centers of flowers and stems. Cut leaves from remainder of candy.

○ *Time-saver Tip:* Substitute 1 package (16 ounces) white angel food cake mix for the Angel Food Cake Deluxe. Prepare and bake as directed on package. Substitute 1 package (7.2 ounces) fluffy white frosting mix for the Lemon Fluff. Prepare as directed on package except stir in 1 tablespoon finely shredded lemon peel and 10 drops yellow food color after beating.

Lemony Date Cake

*Date Chiffon Cake
(below)
Lemon Swirl Frosting
(below)*

*Lemon Twists (below)
Dates, cut into fans*

Bake Date Chiffon Cake as directed. Remove cake from pan. Frost with Lemon Swirl Frosting. Decorate with Lemon Twists and dates. Refrigerate any remaining cake. 12 to 16 servings.

Date Chiffon Cake

*¾ cup boiling water
1 cup finely cut-up
   dates
2 cups all-purpose
   flour
1½ cups sugar
3 teaspoons baking
   powder
1 teaspoon salt*

*½ cup vegetable oil
2 teaspoons finely
   shredded lemon peel
7 egg yolks
1 cup egg whites
   (about 8)
½ teaspoon cream of
   tartar*

Heat oven to 325°. Pour boiling water on dates; let stand until cool. Mix flour, sugar, baking powder and salt. Beat in date mixture, oil, lemon peel and egg yolks with spoon until smooth. Beat egg whites and cream of tartar in large bowl on medium speed until stiff peaks form. Pour egg yolk mixture gradually over beaten egg whites, folding with rubber spatula just until blended. Pour into ungreased tube pan, 10 × 4 inches.

Bake until top springs back when touched lightly, about 1¼ hours. Invert pan on heatproof funnel; let hang until cake is cold.

Lemon Swirl Frosting

*4 cups powdered sugar
½ cup margarine or
   butter, softened
1 package (3 ounces)
   cream cheese,
   softened*

*2 to 3 teaspoons finely
   shredded lemon peel
1 teaspoon vanilla
About 2 tablespoons
   lemon juice*

Beat all ingredients until frosting is fluffy and spreading consistency. If necessary, stir in additional lemon juice, 1 teaspoon at a time.

Lemon Twists

Cut strips from peel of lemon, using small sharp knife. If necessary, trim sides of strips to make even; twist strips into spiral shapes.

Mahogany Pinwheel Cake

*Chocolate Chiffon Cake
(below)*

*Chocolate Glaze (below)
White Glaze (below)*

Bake Chocolate Chiffon Cake as directed. Remove cake from pan. Spread with Chocolate Glaze, letting it run down side unevenly. Using a teaspoon and turning plate as you work, drizzle White Glaze in circles, beginning with small circle in center and encircling with larger circles ½ inch apart. Immediately draw a knife from the center outward 8 times, equally spaced, dividing into 8 equal parts (see page 124). 12 to 16 servings.

Chocolate Chiffon Cake

*¾ cup boiling water
½ cup cocoa
1½ cups all-purpose
   flour or 1¾ cups
   cake flour
1¾ cups sugar
1½ teaspoons baking
   soda*

*1 teaspoon salt
½ cup vegetable oil
2 teaspoons vanilla
7 egg yolks
1 cup egg whites
   (about 8)
½ teaspoon cream of
   tartar*

Heat oven to 325°. Mix boiling water and cocoa; let stand until cool. Mix flour, sugar, baking soda and salt. Beat in cocoa mixture, oil, vanilla and egg yolks with spoon until smooth. Beat egg whites and cream of tartar in large bowl on medium speed until stiff peaks form. Pour egg yolk mixture gradually over beaten egg whites, folding with rubber spatula just until blended. Pour into ungreased tube pan, 10 × 4 inches.

Bake until top springs back when touched lightly, about 1¼ hours. Invert pan on heatproof funnel; let hang until cake is cold.

Chocolate Glaze

Heat 1 package (6 ounces) semisweet chocolate chips, ¼ cup margarine or butter and 2 tablespoons light corn syrup over low heat, stirring constantly, until chocolate is melted. Cool slightly.

White Glaze

Mix ¼ cup powdered sugar and 1 to 2 teaspoons hot water until smooth and desired consistency.

Lemony Date Cake, top, Mahogany Pinwheel Cake, bottom

Mocha-Rum Cream Cake

Chiffon Cake (below)
Mocha Rum Cream
  (right) ·

2/3 cup chopped natural
  almonds, toasted
Chocolate Buttercream
  Frosting (right)

Bake Chiffon Cake as directed. Remove cake from pan; place cake upside down. Slice off top of cake about 1 inch down as shown in diagram and reserve. Cut down into cake 1 inch from outer edge and 1 inch from edge of hole, leaving substantial "walls" on each side. Remove center with a spoon or curved knife, being careful to leave a base of cake 1 inch thick. Prepare Mocha Rum Cream; fold in ⅓ cup of the almonds. Spoon mixture into cake cavity. Replace top of cake and press gently.

Reserve ½ cup Chocolate Buttercream Frosting for a rose; frost cake with remaining frosting. Sprinkle top with remaining almonds. Refrigerate at least 4 hours. Place reserved frosting in decorating bag with petal tip #127. Make 1 large rose (see page 10)

Place rose in desired position on cake. Refrigerate any remaining cake. 12 to 16 servings.

Chiffon Cake

2 cups all-purpose
  flour
1½ cups sugar
3 teaspoons baking
  powder
1 teaspoon salt
¾ cup cold water
½ cup vegetable oil

2 teaspoons finely
  shredded lemon peel
2 teaspoons vanilla
7 egg yolks
1 cup egg whites
  (about 8)
½ teaspoon cream of
  tartar

Heat oven to 325°. Mix flour, sugar, baking powder and salt. Beat in water, oil, lemon peel, vanilla and egg yolks with spoon until smooth. Beat egg whites and cream of tartar in large bowl on medium speed until stiff peaks form. Pour egg yolk mixture gradually over beaten egg whites, folding with rubber spatula just until blended. Pour into ungreased tube pan, 10 × 4 inches.

Bake until top springs back when touched lightly, about 1¼ hours. Invert pan on heatproof funnel; let hang until cake is cold.

Mocha Rum Cream

1 cup chilled whipping
  cream
½ cup powdered sugar
¼ cup cocoa

1 teaspoon instant
  powdered coffee
1 teaspoon rum flavoring

Beat all ingredients except rum flavoring in chilled bowl until stiff. Fold in rum flavoring.

Chocolate Buttercream Frosting

2⅔ cups powdered sugar
⅓ cup margarine or
  butter, softened
⅓ cup shortening

2 ounces melted
  unsweetened
  chocolate (cool)
¾ teapoon vanilla
2 tablespoons milk

Beat all ingredients on medium speed until frosting is smooth and spreading consistency. If necessary, stir in additional milk, ½ teaspoon at a time.

Cutting and Filling Mocha-Rum Cream Cake

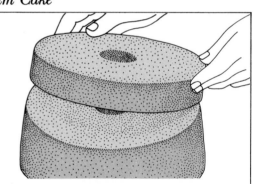

Slice off top of cake about 1 inch down.

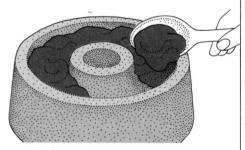

Cut into cake 1 inch from edge and 1 inch from hole. Spoon half of the filling into cavity of cake.

*Mocha-Rum Cream Cake, top,
Chocolate-Almond Cake (page 108), bottom*

Chocolate-Almond Cake

Brown Sugar
    Chiffon Cake
    (below)
Chocolate-Almond
    Filling (right)
1½ cups chilled
    whipping cream

⅓ cup powdered sugar
2 to 3 tablespoons
    almond-flavored
    liqueur
Chocolate Cut-outs
    (right)

Bake Brown Sugar Chiffon Cake as directed. Remove cake from pan. Split cake to make 4 layers (see page 13). Fill each layer with 1 cup Chocolate-Almond Filling. Beat whipping cream and powdered sugar in chilled bowl until stiff; fold in liqueur. Frost cake with whipped cream mixture. Decorate with Chocolate Cut-outs. Refrigerate any remaining cake. 12 to 16 servings

Brown Sugar Chiffon Cake

2 cups all-purpose flour
¾ cup granulated sugar
¾ cup packed brown
    sugar
3 teaspoons baking
    powder
1 teaspoon salt
¾ cup cold water

½ cup vegetable oil
2 teaspoons vanilla
7 egg yolks
1 cup egg whites
    (about 8)
½ teaspoon cream of
    tartar

Heat oven to 325°. Mix flour, sugars, baking powder and salt. Beat in water, oil, vanilla and egg yolks with spoon until smooth. Beat egg whites and cream of tartar in large bowl on medium speed until stiff peaks form. Pour egg yolk mixture gradually over beaten egg whites, folding with rubber spatula just until blended. Pour into ungreased tube pan, 10 × 4 inches.

Bake until top springs back when touched lightly, about 1¼ hours. Invert on heatproof funnel; let hang until cake is cold.

Chocolate-Almond Filling

⅓ cup sugar
3 tablespoons cornstarch
¼ teaspoon salt
2 cups milk
2 ounces unsweetened
    chocolate, cut up

2 egg yolks, slightly
    beaten
2 tablespoons margarine
    or butter
2 tablespoons almond-
    flavored liqueur
2 teaspoons vanilla

Mix sugar, cornstarch and salt in saucepan. Stir in milk gradually; add chocolate. Cook over medium heat, stirring constantly, until chocolate is melted. Stir at least half of the hot mixture gradually into egg yolks. Blend into hot mixture in saucepan. Heat to boiling, stirring constantly. Boil and stir 2 minutes. Stir in margarine, liqueur and vanilla. Cover surface of pudding with plastic wrap; cool.

Chocolate Cut-outs

Heat 1 bar (4 ounces) sweet cooking chocolate over low heat until melted. Spread over outside bottom of square pan, 8 × 8 × 2 inches. Before chocolate hardens, pull fork or decorating comb gently across surface for rippled effect. Refrigerate until firm; bring to room temperature. Cut into circles, diamonds, stars or other desired shapes. Refrigerate until ready to use.

TWO QUICK DECORATING TRICKS

For a frosting flower design, frost cake with a fluffy frosting, reserving ¾ to 1 cup frosting. Tint reserved frosting as desired. Drop 5 to 8 mounds of tinted frosting around center of cake; draw out with spoon to make petals. Add 5 to 8 smaller mounds for second layer of petals, pulling tips up with back of spoon. Pull frosting up to shape center.

Mark the frosting of an 8- or 9-inch square cake into nine squares with a knife or wooden pick. Fill the squares with chopped nuts, miniature chocolate chips, confetti candy bits, chocolate shot, tinted coconut, colored sugars, crushed peppermint candy, multicolored chocolate-covered candies or toasted oat cereal.

Orange-Lemon Refrigerator Cake

*Chiffon Layer Cake
(below)*
*Orange-Lemon Filling
(right)*
*1 cup chilled whipping
cream*

¼ cup powdered sugar
*1 teaspoon finely
shredded orange peel*
*Orange Peel Tulip
(right)*

Bake Chiffon Layer Cake as directed. Remove cake from pans. Split cake to make 4 layers (see page 12). Fill each layer and frost top of cake with about ½ cup Orange-Lemon Filling. Wrap in plastic wrap or aluminum foil. Refrigerate at least 12 hours.

Just before serving, beat whipping cream and powdered sugar in chilled bowl until stiff; fold in orange peel. Frost cake with whipped cream mixture. Decorate with Orange Peel Tulip. Refrigerate any remaining cake. 10 to 14 servings.

Chiffon Layer Cake

*1 cup plus 2 tablespoons
  all-purpose flour*
1 cup sugar
*2 teaspoons baking
  powder*
¾ teaspoon salt
½ cup cold water

⅓ cup vegetable oil
3 egg yolks
*⅔ cup egg whites
  (about 6)*
*½ teaspoon cream of
  tartar*

Heat oven to 350°. Mix flour, sugar, baking powder and salt. Beat in water, oil and egg yolks with spoon until smooth. Beat egg whites and cream of tartar in large bowl on medium speed until stiff peaks form. Pour egg yolk mixture gradually over beaten egg whites, folding with rubber spatula just until blended. Pour into 2 ungreased round pans, 8 or 9 × 1½ inches.

Bake until top springs back when touched lightly in center, 30 to 35 minutes. Invert pans with edges on 2 other pans; let hang until layers are cold.

Orange-Lemon Filling

½ cup sugar
3 tablespoons cornstarch
⅛ teaspoon salt
1 cup orange juice
½ cup water
*2 egg yolks, slightly
  beaten*

2 tablespoons lemon juice
*1 tablespoon finely
  shredded orange peel*
*1 tablespoon margarine
  or butter*

Mix sugar, cornstarch and salt in 2-quart saucepan. Stir in orange juice and water gradually. Cook over medium heat, stirring constantly, until mixture thickens and boils. Boil and stir 1 minute. Stir at least half of the hot mixture gradually into egg yolks. Blend into hot mixture in saucepan. Boil 1 minute, stirring constantly. Remove from heat. Stir in lemon juice, orange peel and margarine. Refrigerate until set, about 1 hour.

Orange Peel Tulip

Cover an orange with hot water; let stand 5 minutes. Cut peel into fourths; remove from orange. Cut white membrane from peel. Cut peel into tulip shape with scissors or sharp knife.

Fruit Savarins

Sponge Cake (below)
Brandy Syrup (below)
1 jar (12 ounces) apricot
    preserves
3 tablespoons lemon juice

Pineapple,
    strawberries,
    blueberries, mandarin
    orange segments

Bake Sponge Cake as directed. Place savarins in jelly roll pan or tray with rim; cool slightly. Prick savarins all over with wooden pick. Drizzle 2 tablespoons Brandy Syrup on each; let stand 15 minutes. Repeat until all syrup is used.

Heat apricot preserves and lemon juice over medium heat, stirring occasionally. Cool slightly; strain. Place savarins on wire rack. Fill centers with fruit. Spoon apricot glaze over savarins and fruit. 16 savarins.

Sponge Cake

1 cup egg whites
    (about 8)
½ teaspoon cream of
    tartar
½ teaspoon salt
1 cup sugar
5 egg yolks

½ cup sugar
1 cup all-purpose flour
2 tablespoons water
½ teaspoon almond
    extract
½ teaspoon lemon extract
½ teaspoon vanilla

Heat oven to 325°. Beat egg whites, cream of tartar and salt in large bowl until foamy. Beat in 1 cup sugar, 1 tablespoon at a time; continue beating until stiff and glossy. Do not underbeat.

Beat egg yolks in small bowl until very thick and lemon colored, about 5 minutes. Beat in ½ cup sugar gradually. Beat in flour alternately with water and flavorings on low speed. Fold egg yolk mixture into meringue. Spoon batter into buttered individual savarin molds, filling each ⅔ full. Place on cookie sheet.

Bake until golden brown, about 20 minutes. Cool 10 minutes; remove from molds.

Brandy Syrup

Heat 1 cup water and ¾ cup sugar to boiling, stirring occasionally. Cool to lukewarm; stir in ¼ cup brandy.

Chocolate Mint Loaves

Peppermint Chiffon Cake
    (below)
Chocolate-Mint Frosting
    (below)

7 to 10 square chocolate
    party mints

Bake Peppermint Chiffon Cake as directed. Remove loaves from pans. Reserve 3 cups Chocolate-Mint Frosting for decorating; frost loaves with remaining frosting. Place reserved frosting in decorating bag with large open star tip #4B. Pipe frosting in continuous motion back and forth across tops of loaves. Cut party mints diagonally into halves if desired; decorate top of cake. Refrigerate any remaining cake. 16 servings.

Peppermint Chiffon Cake

2 cups all-purpose
    flour
1½ cups sugar
3 teaspoons baking
    powder
1 teaspoon salt
¾ cup cold water
½ cup vegetable oil

½ teaspoon peppermint
    extract
7 egg yolks
1 cup egg whites
    (about 8)
½ teaspoon cream of
    tartar

Heat oven to 325°. Mix flour, sugar, baking powder and salt. Beat in water, oil, peppermint extract and egg yolks with spoon until smooth.

Beat egg whites and cream of tartar in large bowl on medium speed until stiff peaks form. Pour egg yolk mixture gradually over beaten egg whites, folding with rubber spatula just until blended. Divide batter between 2 ungreased loaf pans, 9 × 5 × 3 inches.

Bake until top springs back when touched lightly, 50 to 55 minutes. Invert pans with edges on 2 other pans; let hang until cakes are cold.

Chocolate-Mint Frosting

3 cups chilled
    whipping cream
1½ cups powdered sugar

¾ cup cocoa
1½ teaspoons peppermint
    extract

Beat all ingredients in chilled bowl until stiff.

Clockwise from top: Fruit Mosaic Cake (page 112),
Chocolate Mint Loaf, Fruit Savarins

Fruit Mosaic Cake

Hot Water Sponge Cake
  (below)
Cream Cheese Frosting
  (below)

Strawberry halves,
  banana slices, mandarin
  orange segments

Bake Hot Water Sponge Cake as directed. Frost with Cream Cheese Frosting. Decorate with fruit. Refrigerate any remaining cake. 12 servings.

Hot Water Sponge Cake

3 eggs
³/₄ cup sugar
¹/₃ cup hot water
1 teaspoon vanilla
¹/₂ teaspoon lemon extract

1¹/₄ cups cake flour
1¹/₂ teaspoons baking
  powder
¹/₂ teaspoon salt

Heat oven to 350°. Grease and flour square pan, 9×9×2 inches. Beat eggs in small bowl on high speed until very thick and lemon colored, about 5 minutes; pour into large bowl. Beat in sugar gradually. Beat in water, vanilla and lemon extract on medium speed. Add flour, baking powder and salt on medium speed, beating just until batter is smooth. Pour into pan.

Bake until top springs back when touched lightly, 25 to 30 minutes. Cool 10 minutes; remove from pan. Cool completely.

Cream Cheese Frosting

1 package (3 ounces)
  cream cheese, softened

³/₄ cup chilled whipping
  cream
¹/₄ cup powdered sugar
¹/₂ teaspoon vanilla

Beat cream cheese in chilled bowl until smooth. Beat in remaining ingredients on high speed, scraping bowl occasionally, until stiff peaks form.

Caramel-Almond Cake

Marbled Sponge Cake
  (right)
Marshmallow-Orange
  Frosting (right)

¹/₄ cup sliced almonds
  Caramel Almonds
  (right)

Bake Marbled Sponge Cake as directed. Prepare Marshmallow-Orange Frosting. Remove cake from pan. Split to make 3 layers (see page 13). Fold ¹/₄ cup almonds and the reserved raisins from frosting into 1¹/₂ cups of the frosting; fill layers with mixture. Frost cake with remaining frosting. Coat top of cake with Caramel Almonds. Refrigerate any remaining cake. 12 to 16 servings.

Marbled Sponge Cake

1 cup cake flour
³/₄ cup sugar
1¹/₂ cups egg whites
  (about 12)
1¹/₂ teaspoons cream of
  tartar

¹/₄ teaspoon salt
³/₄ cup sugar
1 teaspoon almond
  extract
6 egg yolks

Heat oven to 375°. Mix flour and ³/₄ cup sugar. Beat egg whites, cream of tartar and salt in large bowl on medium speed until foamy. Beat in ³/₄ cup sugar on high speed, 1 tablespoon at a time; continue beating until stiff and glossy. Add almond extract with last addition of sugar. Do not underbeat. Beat egg yolks in small bowl on high speed until very thick and lemon colored, about 5 minutes.

Sprinkle flour-sugar mixture, ¹/₄ cup at a time, over meringue, folding in just until flour-sugar mixture disappears. Pour half of the batter into another bowl; fold in beaten egg yolks. Spoon yellow and white batters alternately into ungreased tube pan, 10×4 inches. Cut gently through batters to swirl.

Bake until top springs back when touched lightly, 60 to 65 minutes. Invert pan on heatproof funnel; let hang until cake is cold.

Marshmallow-Orange Frosting

¹/₄ cup raisins
¹/₄ cup orange-flavored
  liqueur
16 large marshmallows

2 tablespoons shredded
  orange peel
¹/₄ cup orange juice
1¹/₂ cups chilled
  whipping cream

Heat raisins and liqueur over low heat until hot, cool. Drain; reserve liquid. Reserve raisins for filling. Heat reserved liquid, the marshmallows, orange peel and orange juice over medium heat, stirring constantly, just until marshmallows are melted. Refrigerate until thickened. Beat whipping cream in chilled bowl until stiff. Fold marshmallow mixture into whipped cream. Refrigerate 1 hour.

Caramel Almonds

Cook ²/₃ cup sliced almonds in 3 tablespoons packed brown sugar over low heat, stirring constantly, until sugar melts and almonds are coated. Spread on waxed paper-lined cookie sheet. Cool; break apart.

Caramel-Almond Cake, top, Chocolate-Orange Ribbon Torte (page 114), bottom

Chocolate-Orange Ribbon Torte

Chocolate Sponge Cake
(below)
Chocolate-Fruit Filling
(right)

Orange Frosting
(right)
½ ounce melted
unsweetened
chocolate (cool)

Bake Chocolate Sponge Cake as directed. Cut into 4 rectangles, 9¾ × 3½ inches. Alternate cake layers and Chocolate-Fruit Filling, beginning and ending with cake. Reserve 1 cup Orange Frosting for decorating; frost torte with remaining frosting.

Stir chocolate into reserved frosting; place in decorating bag with open star tip #18. Pipe zigzag border (see page 9) around base and top edge of torte; pipe rope design in crisscross fashion on top and side of torte. Decorate with candied fruit if desired. Refrigerate any remaining torte. 10 to 12 servings.

Chocolate Sponge Cake

3 eggs
1 cup granulated sugar
⅓ cup water
1 teaspoon vanilla
¾ cup all-purpose flour

¼ cup cocoa
1 teaspoon baking
    powder
¼ teaspoon salt
    Powdered sugar

Heat oven to 375°. Line jelly roll pan, 15½ × 10½ × 1 inch with aluminum foil; grease generously. Beat eggs in small bowl on high speed until very thick and lemon colored, about 5 minutes; pour into large bowl. Beat in granulated sugar gradually. Beat in water and vanilla on medium speed. Add flour, cocoa, baking powder and salt gradually, beating just until batter is smooth. Pour into pan.

Bake until wooden pick inserted in center comes out clean, 12 to 15 minutes. Immediately loosen cake from edges of pan; invert on towel sprinkled generously with powdered sugar. Carefully remove foil. Trim off stiff edges if necessary. Cool on wire rack at least 30 minutes.

Chocolate-Fruit Filling

1 carton (about 16
    ounces) dry ricotta
    cheese
¼ cup sugar
2 tablespoons milk
2 tablespoons
    orange-flavored
    liqueur

¼ teaspoon salt
⅓ cup semisweet
    chocolate chips,
    chopped
⅓ cup finely chopped
    mixed candied fruit

Beat all ingredients except chocolate chips and candied fruit in small bowl on medium speed until smooth, 2 to 3 minutes. Stir in chocolate chips and candied fruit.

Orange Frosting

3½ cups powdered sugar
⅔ cup all-purpose flour
½ cup margarine or
    butter, softened
¼ teaspoon salt
1 teaspoon finely
    shredded orange
    peel

2 tablespoons orange
    juice
1 tablespoon light corn
    syrup
2 tablespoons water

Beat all ingredients on medium speed until frosting is smooth and spreading consistency. If necessary, stir in additional water, ½ teaspoon at a time.

Storing Cakes

Cool unfrosted cakes completely before storing. If covered warm, they become sticky.

Store cake with a creamy-type frosting under a cake safe (or large inverted bowl) or cover loosely with aluminum foil, plastic wrap or waxed paper.

Cakes with whipped cream toppings or cream fillings should be stored in the refrigerator.

Because so much air is incorporated into fluffy frostings, they are not as stable as creamy frostings. It is best to serve a cake with fluffy frosting on the day it is made.

However, if you must store the cake overnight, place it under a cake safe or inverted bowl but slip a knife blade under the rim so the cover is not airtight.

Sacher Cake Roll

Chocolate Cake Roll
(below)
1 jar (12 ounces) apricot
preserves

Chocolate Glaze (below)
Decorators' Chocolate
(below)

Bake Chocolate Cake Roll as directed. Unroll cake; remove towel. Spread ⅔ cup of the apricot preserves over cake; roll up. Heat remaining preserves just to boiling; strain. Pour apricot glaze over top and sides of roll. Let stand until set. Spread with Chocolate Glaze. Place Decorators' Chocolate in decorating bag with writing tip #3. Pipe bows onto cake roll as shown in photograph. 10 servings.

Chocolate Cake Roll

3 eggs
1 cup granulated sugar
⅓ cup water
1 teaspoon vanilla
¾ cup all-purpose flour

¼ cup cocoa
1 teaspoon baking
powder
¼ teaspoon salt
Powdered sugar

Heat oven to 375°. Line jelly roll pan, 15½ × 10½ × 1 inch, with aluminum foil; grease generously. Beat eggs in small bowl on high speed until very thick and lemon colored, about 5 minutes; pour into large bowl. Beat in granulated sugar gradually. Beat in water and vanilla on low speed. Add flour, cocoa, baking powder and salt gradually, beating just until batter is smooth. Pour into pan.

Bake until wooden pick inserted in center comes out clean, 12 to 15 minutes. Immediately loosen cake from edges of pan; invert on towel sprinkled generously with powdered sugar. Carefully remove foil. Trim off stiff edges if necessary. While hot, carefully roll cake and towel from narrow end. Cool on wire rack at least 30 minutes.

Chocolate Glaze

Heat ½ cup semisweet chocolate chips, 2 tablespoons margarine or butter and 1 tablespoon light corn syrup over low heat, stirring constantly, until chocolate is melted. Cool slightly.

Decorators' Chocolate

Heat 1 square (1 ounce) unsweetened chocolate and 1 teaspoon shortening over low heat until chocolate is melted. Remove from heat. Stir in 1 to 2 tablespoons powdered sugar, 1 teaspoon at a time, until chocolate is desired consistency.

Sacher Cake Roll

Lemon Dessert Roll

Lemon Dessert Roll

Lemon Filling (right)   *Lemon Rose (right)*
Cake Roll (right)   *Mint leaf, if desired*
Meringue (right)

Prepare Lemon Filling. Bake Cake Roll as directed.

Heat oven to 400°. Unroll cake; remove towel. Reserve ½ cup filling for decorating; spread remaining filling over cake. Roll up. Place on ungreased cookie sheet. Spread with Meringue. Make 3 strips lengthwise across Meringue with small metal spatula. Bake until delicate brown, 8 to 10 minutes. Fill strips with reserved filling. Decorate with Lemon Rose and mint leaf. Refrigerate any remaining cake roll. 10 servings.

Lemon Filling

1 cup sugar	1 tablespoon margarine
¼ cup cornstarch	or butter
¼ teaspoon salt	1 tablespoon plus 1½
1 cup water	teaspoons finely
3 egg yolks, slightly	shredded lemon peel
beaten	½ cup lemon juice

Mix sugar, cornstarch and salt in saucepan. Stir in water gradually. Cook, stirring constantly, until mixture thickens and boils. Boil and stir 1 minute. Stir half of the hot mixture gradually into egg yolks; blend into hot mixture in saucepan. Boil and stir 1 minute. Remove from heat; stir in margarine, lemon peel and lemon juice. Cool until set.

Cake Roll

3 eggs	1 teaspoon baking
1 cup granulated sugar	powder
⅓ cup water	¼ teapsoon salt
1 teaspoon vanilla	Powdered sugar
¾ cup all-purpose flour	

Heat oven to 375°. Line jelly roll pan, 15½ × 10½ × 1 inch, with aluminum foil; grease generously. Beat eggs in small bowl on high speed until very thick and lemon colored, about 5 minutes; pour into large bowl. Beat in granulated sugar gradually. Beat in water and vanilla on low speed. Add flour, baking powder and salt gradually, beating just until batter is smooth. Pour into pan.

Bake until wooden pick inserted in center comes out clean, 12 to 15 minutes. Immediately loosen cake from edges of pan; invert on towel sprinkled generously with powdered sugar. Carefully remove foil. Trim off stiff edges if necessary. While hot, carefully roll cake and towel from narrow end. Cool on wire rack at least 30 minutes.

Meringue

Beat 2 egg whites until foamy. Beat 1 cup sugar and 1 tablespoon lemon juice gradually into egg whites until stiff.

Lemon Rose

Cut thin slice from stem end of lemon. Starting just above cut end, cut around lemon in a continuous motion to form a spiral of peel. Carefully curl peel spiral to resemble a rose.

Mocha Ice Cream Roll, left, Wine Cream Roll, right

Mocha Ice Cream Roll

*Chocolate Cake Roll
    (page 115)*
*1 to 1½ pints coffee-
    flavored ice cream*

*Powdered sugar
Chocolate-Rum Sauce
    (below)*

Bake Chocolate Cake Roll as directed. Soften ice cream slightly. Unroll cake; remove towel. Spread ice cream over cake. Roll up; wrap in plastic wrap. Freeze several hours until firm. Place ¾-inch strips of waxed paper diagonally across roll. Press powdered sugar through sieve onto roll; carefully remove waxed paper strips. Serve with Chocolate-Rum Sauce. 10 servings.

Chocolate-Rum Sauce

*1 can (13 ounces)
    evaporated milk*
2 cups sugar
*4 squares (1 ounce each)
    unsweetened chocolate*

*¼ cup margarine or
    butter*
*2 tablespoons dark rum
    or 2 teaspoons rum
    flavoring*
½ teaspoon salt

Heat evaporated milk and sugar over medium heat, stirring constantly, to rolling boil. Boil and stir 1 minute. Add chocolate; stir until melted. Beat over medium heat until smooth. Remove from heat; stir in margarine, rum and salt. Refrigerate any remaining sauce.

Wine Cream Roll

Cake Roll (page 116)
⅓ cup granulated sugar
*1 tablespoon plus 1
    teaspoon cornstarch*
1 cup dry white wine
2 eggs, slightly beaten

*3 tablespoons margarine
    or butter*
*Powdered sugar
Strawberry Sauce
    (below)*

Bake Cake Roll as directed. Mix ⅓ cup granulated sugar and the cornstarch in saucepan; stir in wine. Cook over medium heat, stirring constantly, until mixture thickens and boils. Boil and stir 1 minute. Stir half of the hot mixture gradually into beaten eggs; blend into hot mixture in saucepan. Boil and stir 1 minute. Remove from heat; stir in margarine. Refrigerate until cool. Unroll cake; remove towel. Spread filling over cake to within ¼ inch of edges; roll up. Refrigerate at least 1 hour.

Press powdered sugar through sieve onto roll; (see Mocha Ice Cream Roll, left) serve with Strawberry Sauce. Refrigerate any remaining roll. 10 servings.

Strawberry Sauce

*1 package (10 ounces)
    frozen strawberries,
    thawed and drained
    (reserve 2 tablespoons
    syrup)*

*1 jar (10 ounces)
    currant jelly*
2 tablespoons cornstarch
1 tablespoon lemon juice

Heat strawberries and jelly to boiling. Mix cornstarch and reserved strawberry syrup; stir into strawberries. Heat to boiling, stirring constantly. Boil and stir 2 minutes. Remove from heat; stir in lemon juice. Cool slightly.

Mocha Velvet Cream Cake

*Black Midnight Cake
  (below)*
*Mocha Whipped Cream
  (right)*
Chocolate Glaze (right)
Chopped almonds

Bake Black Midnight Cake as directed. Split cake horizontally to make 4 layers (see page 12). Fill each layer with about 1 cup Mocha Whipped Cream. Spread top of cake with Chocolate Glaze, letting it run down side unevenly. Sprinkle chopped almonds around top edge of cake. Refrigerate any remaining cake. 14 to 16 servings.

Black Midnight Cake

2¼ cups all-purpose flour or cake flour	1¼ teaspoons baking soda
1⅔ cups sugar	1 teaspoon salt
¾ cup shortening	¼ teaspoon baking powder
⅔ cup cocoa	1 teaspoon vanilla
1¼ cups water	2 eggs

Heat oven to 350°. Grease and flour 2 round pans, 9 × 1½ inches. Beat all ingredients in large bowl on medium speed, scraping bowl constantly, until blended, about 30 seconds. Beat on high speed, scraping bowl occasionally, 3 minutes. Pour batter into pans.

Bake until wooden pick inserted in center comes out clean, 30 to 35 minutes. Cool 10 minutes; remove from pans. Cool completely.

Mocha Whipped Cream

1½ cups chilled whipping cream	2 tablespoons cocoa
⅓ cup powdered sugar	2 teaspoons instant coffee

Beat all ingredients in chilled bowl until stiff.

Chocolate Glaze

2 tablespoons cocoa	1 tablespoon water
2 tablespoons margarine or butter	1 tablespoon corn syrup
	1 cup powdered sugar

Heat cocoa, margarine, water and corn syrup in 1½-quart saucepan over low heat, stirring constantly, just until margarine is melted. Remove from heat; stir in powdered sugar. If necessary, stir in additional water, ½ teaspoon at a time, until desired consistency.

○ *Time-saver Tip:* Substitute 1 package (18.5 ounces) devils food or chocolate fudge cake mix with pudding for the Black Midnight Cake. Prepare and bake as directed on package.

Mocha Velvet Cream Cake

Deluxe Chocolate Cake

Sour Cream Chocolate
Cake (below)

Sour Cream Chocolate
Frosting (below)
Chocolate Curls (right)

Bake Sour Cream Chocolate Cake as directed. Fill layers and frost side of cake with Sour Cream Chocolate Frosting; spread thin layer of frosting on top of cake. Draw decorating comb around side of cake if desired.

Place remaining frosting in decorating bag with petal tip #127 or large open star tip #8. Hold bag at 45° angle with wide end of tip down. Pipe border around top edge of cake in up and down motion to form ruffle; repeat in parallel circles, working toward center of cake, until all of the frosting has been used. Carefully place Chocolate Curls in center. 14 to 16 servings.

Sour Cream Chocolate Cake

2 cups all-purpose flour	1 teaspoon salt
2 cups sugar	½ teaspoon baking powder
¾ cup dairy sour cream	1 teaspoon vanilla
¼ cup shortening	2 eggs
1 cup water	4 ounces melted unsweetened chocolate (cool)
1¼ teaspoons baking soda	

Heat oven to 350°. Grease and flour 2 round pans, 9 × 1½ inches, or 3 round pans, 8 × 1½ inches. Beat all ingredients in large bowl on medium speed, scraping bowl constantly, until blended, about 30 seconds. Beat on high speed, scraping bowl occasionally, 3 minutes. Pour into pans.

Bake until wooden pick inserted in center comes out clean, 30 to 35 minutes. Cool 10 minutes; remove from pans. Cool completely.

Sour Cream Chocolate Frosting

¾ cup dairy sour cream	3 ounces melted unsweetened chocolate (cool)
½ cup margarine or butter, softened	2 teaspoons vanilla
	5 cups powdered sugar

Mix sour cream, margarine, chocolate and vanilla. Stir in powdered sugar; beat just until frosting is smooth and spreading consistency. If necessary, stir in additional powdered sugar.

Chocolate Curls

Place bar of milk chocolate on waxed paper. Make chocolate curls by pressing firmly against the chocolate and pulling a vegetable parer toward you as shown in diagram. Transfer each curl carefully with a wooden pick to avoid breaking.

TIPS: The curls will be easier to make if the chocolate is slightly warm. Let the chocolate stand in a warm place for about 15 minutes before slicing. Semisweet chocolate can be used but curls will be smaller. Thicker bars of chocolate will make larger curls.

○ *Time-saver Tip:* Substitute 1 package (18.5 ounces) devils food or chocolate fudge cake mix with pudding for the Sour Cream Chocolate Cake. Prepare and bake as directed on package for two 8- or 9-inch layers.

Chocolate Curls

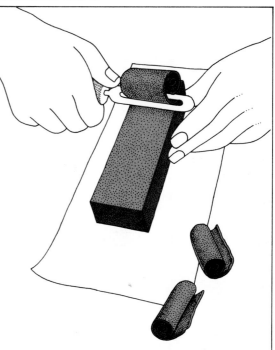

Make curls by pressing vegetable parer firmly against bar of chocolate and pulling parer toward you in long, thin strokes.

Creamy Cherry Cake

Creamy Cherry Cake

Maraschino Cherry Cake
  (below)

Creamy Cherry Frosting
  (right)

Bake Maraschino Cherry Cake as directed. Reserve 1½ cups Creamy Cherry Frosting for decorating; fill layers and frost cake with remaining frosting. Place reserved frosting in decorating bag with open star tip #18. Pipe shell border around base of cake (see page 9). Using same tip, pipe drop flowers onto side and top of cake (see page 8). 12 to 16 servings.

Maraschino Cherry Cake

2¼ cups all-purpose flour	3½ teaspoons baking powder
1⅔ cups sugar	1 teaspoon salt
⅔ cup shortening	5 egg whites
¾ cup milk	½ cup chopped nuts
½ cup maraschino cherry juice	16 maraschino cherries, cut into eighths

Heat oven to 350°. Grease and flour 2 round pans, 9 × 1½ inches. Beat flour, sugar, shortening, milk, cherry juice, baking powder and salt in large bowl on medium speed, scraping bowl constantly, until blended, about 30 seconds. Beat on high speed, scraping bowl occasionally, 2 minutes. Beat in egg whites on high speed, scraping bowl occasionally, 2 minutes. Fold in nuts and cherries. Pour into pans.

Bake until wooden pick inserted in center comes out clean, 30 to 35 minutes. Cool 10 minutes; remove from pans. Cool completely.

Creamy Cherry Frosting

4 cups powdered sugar	1 teaspoon almond extract
½ cup margarine or butter, softened	⅛ teaspoon red food color
½ cup shortening	1 tablespoon milk
3 tablespoons maraschino cherry juice	

Beat all ingredients on medium speed until frosting is smooth and spreading consistency. If necessary, stir in additional milk, 1 teaspoon at a time.

○ *Time-saver Tip:* Substitute 1 package (18.5 ounces) white cake mix with pudding for the Maraschino Cherry Cake. Prepare and bake as directed on package except stir ½ cup finely chopped nuts and ½ cup finely chopped maraschino cherries, well drained, into batter.

Pineapple Cream Cake

Rum-flavored Cake
(below)
Pineapple Cream Filling
(right)
Cream Cheese Frosting
(right)

2 drops yellow food color
Pineapple slices, well
drained
Green food color

Bake Rum-flavored Cake as directed. Split cake to make 4 layers (see page 12); fill layers with Pineapple Cream Filling. Reserve ¾ cup Cream Cheese Frosting for decorating; frost cake with remaining frosting. Make vertical lines on side of cake with decorating comb or tines of fork if desired. Stir yellow food color into reserved frosting; place in decorating bag with open star tip #18. Pipe scrolls around top edge of cake.

Cut pineapple slices into 1-inch wedges and place above scroll design for base of pineapple. Cut another pineapple slice into ½-inch wedges. Tint green in mixture of few drops green food color and few drops water; drain well. Cut 3 slashes in wide end of green wedges; spread slightly. Place on pineapple bases on cake. Refrigerate any remaining cake. 10 to 14 servings.

Rum-flavored Cake

2¼ cups all-purpose
flour
1⅔ cups sugar
⅔ cup shortening
1¼ cups milk

3½ teaspoons baking
powder
1 teaspoon salt
1 teaspoon rum
flavoring
5 egg whites

Heat oven to 350°. Grease and flour 2 round pans, 8 × 1½ inches. Beat flour, sugar, shortening, milk, baking powder, salt and rum flavoring in large bowl on medium speed, scraping bowl constantly, until blended, about 30 seconds. Beat on high speed, scraping bowl occasionally, 2 minutes. Beat in egg whites on high speed, scraping bowl occasionally, 2 minutes. Pour into pans.

Bake until wooden pick inserted in center comes out clean, 35 to 40 minutes. Cool 10 minutes; remove from pans. Cool completely.

Pineapple Cream Filling

2 tablespoons sugar
1 tablespoon cornstarch
1 cup milk
1 can (8 ounces) crushed
pineapple, undrained

4 egg yolks, slightly
beaten
1 teaspoon finely
shredded lemon peel

Mix sugar and cornstarch in saucepan. Stir in milk and pineapple gradually. Cook over medium heat, stirring constantly, until mixture thickens and boils. Boil and stir 1 minute. Remove from heat. Stir at least half of the hot mixture gradually into egg yolks. Blend into hot mixture in saucepan. Boil and stir 1 minute; remove from heat. Stir in the lemon peel; cool.

Cream Cheese Frosting

6 cups powdered sugar
1½ packages (3 ounces
each) cream cheese,
softened

¾ cup margarine or
butter, softened
⅛ teaspoon salt
1½ teaspoons vanilla
3 tablespoons milk

Beat all ingredients on medium speed until frosting is smooth and spreading consistency. If necessary, stir in additional milk, 1 teaspoon at a time.

○ *Time-saver Tip:* Substitute 1 package (18.5 ounces) white cake mix with pudding for the Rum-flavored Cake. Prepare and bake as directed on the package.

TWO QUICK DECORATING TRICKS

Frost a rectangular or round layer cake with a fluffy frosting. Drizzle chocolate-flavored syrup in thin lines diagonally across the frosting at about 1-inch intervals. Draw a knife or the side of a small metal spatula diagonally in one direction across the lines of syrup at 1-inch intervals.

Frost one half of a rectangular cake with a dark frosting and one half with a light frosting. Thin the remaining frostings with a small amount of water and drizzle opposite frostings over opposite sides of cake.

Lemon Allegretti Cake

Classic White Cake   White Mountain
  (below)   Frosting (page 16)
Lemon Filling (page 67)   2 teaspoons hot water

Bake Classic White Cake as directed. Split cake to make 4 layers (see page 12). Reserve ¼ cup Lemon Filling for decorating; fill layers with remaining filling. Frost cake with White Mountain Frosting.

Mix reserved filling and hot water. If necessary, stir in additional hot water, ½ teaspoon at a time, until desired consistency. Using a teaspoon, drizzle filling around top edge of cake, letting it run down side unevenly. Decorate with 1 to 3 yellow Sugared Roses (see page 74) if desired. 10 to 14 servings.

Classic White Cake

2¼ cups all-purpose   3½ teaspoons baking
     flour   powder
1⅔ cups sugar   1 teaspoon salt
  ⅔ cup shortening   1 teaspoon vanilla
1¼ cups milk   5 egg whites

Heat oven to 350°. Grease and flour 2 round pans, 8 or 9 × 1½ inches. Beat flour, sugar, shortening, milk, baking powder, salt and vanilla in large bowl on medium speed, scraping bowl constantly, until blended, about 30 seconds. Beat on high speed, scraping bowl occasionally, 2 minutes. Beat in egg whites on high speed, scraping bowl occasionally, 2 minutes. Pour into pans.

Bake until wooden pick inserted in center comes out clean, 30 to 35 minutes. Cool 10 minutes; remove from pans. Cool completely.

○ *Time-saver Tip:* Substitute 1 package (18.5 ounces) white cake mix with pudding for the Classic White Cake. Prepare and bake as directed on package. Substitute 1 package (7.2 ounces) fluffy white frosting mix for the White Mountain Frosting. Prepare as directed on package.

Clockwise from top: Geometric Flower Cake (page 124), Pineapple Cream Cake (page 121), Lemon Allegretti Cake

Geometric Flower Cake

*Almond White Cake
(below)*
*Sour Cream-Raisin
Filling (below)*

*Seven Minute Frosting
(right)*
*1 ounce melted
unsweetened chocolate
(cool)*

Bake Almond White Cake as directed. Split to make 4 layers (see page 12). Fill layers with Sour Cream-Raisin Filling. Frost cake with Seven Minute Frosting. Immediately pour chocolate on frosting, beginning with small circle in center and encircling with larger circles 1 inch apart. Draw a knife from center outward and from outside edge inward alternately, 8 times, dividing into 8 equal parts. Refrigerate any remaining cake. 10 to 14 servings.

Almond White Cake

*2¼ cups all-purpose
 flour*
1⅔ cups sugar
⅔ cup shortening
1¼ cups milk

*3½ teaspoons baking
 powder*
1 teaspoon salt
*1 teaspoon almond
 extract*
5 egg whites

Heat oven to 350°. Grease and flour 2 round pans, 8 or 9 × 1½ inches. Beat flour, sugar, shortening, milk, baking powder, salt and almond extract in large bowl on medium speed, scraping bowl constantly, until blended, about 30 seconds. Beat on high speed, scraping bowl occasionally, 2 minutes. Beat in egg whites on high speed, scraping bowl occasionally, 2 minutes. Pour into pans.

Bake until wooden pick inserted in center comes out clean, 30 to 35 minutes. Cool 10 minutes; remove from pans. Cool completely.

Sour Cream-Raisin Filling

*¾ cup granulated
 sugar*
*¾ cup packed brown
 sugar*
*3 tablespoons
 cornstarch*

*1½ cups dairy sour
 cream*
2 eggs
1 cup golden raisins
½ cup chopped walnuts
1 teaspoon vanilla

Mix sugars and cornstarch in saucepan; stir in sour cream and eggs. Cook over medium heat, stirring constantly, until mixture thickens and boils. Boil and stir 1 minute; remove from heat. Stir in raisins, walnuts and vanilla; cool.

Seven Minute Frosting

1½ cups sugar
*¼ teaspoon cream of
 tartar*
⅓ cup water

2 egg whites
*1 tablespoon light corn
 syrup*
1 teaspoon vanilla

Beat all ingredients except vanilla in top of double boiler on high speed 1 minute. Place over boiling water; beat on high speed until stiff peaks form, about 7 minutes. Remove from heat; add vanilla. Beat on high speed 2 minutes.

○ *Time-saver Tip:* Substitute 1 package (18.5 ounces) white cake mix with pudding for the Almond White Cake. Prepare and bake as directed on package except add 1 teaspoon almond extract before beating. Substitute 1 package (7.2 ounces) fluffy white frosting mix for the Seven Minute Frosting. Prepare as directed on package.

Making Geometric Design

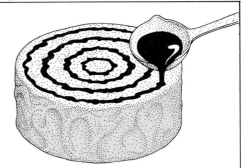

Pour chocolate on frosting, beginning with small circle in center and encircling with larger circles 1 inch apart.

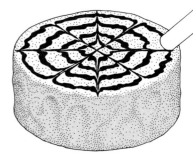

Draw a spatula or knife from center outward and from outside inward alternately, 8 times.

Buttercream Pecan Cake

White Pecan Cake (below)   Buttercream Frosting
Mocha Butter Frosting   (right)
  (right)   12 pecan halves

Bake White Pecan Cake as directed. Fill layers and
frost cake with Mocha Butter Frosting. Place
Buttercream Frosting in decorating bag with open
star tip #32. Pipe 5 lines at equal intervals across
top of cake, 3 lengthwise and 2 crosswise. Place
pecan half in each of the 12 squares. Pipe border
around base and top edge of cake. 12 servings.

White Pecan Cake

2¼ cups all-purpose   1¼ cups milk
   flour   3½ teaspoons baking
1⅔ cups sugar   powder
  1 cup chopped pecans   1 teaspoon salt
⅔ cup shortening (half   1 teaspoon vanilla
   margarine or   5 egg whites
   butter, softened)

Heat oven to 350°. Grease and flour 2 square pans,
8 × 8 × 2 inches. Beat flour, sugar, pecans, shortening, milk, baking powder, salt and vanilla in large
bowl on medium speed, scraping bowl constantly,
until blended, about 30 seconds. Beat on high
speed, scraping bowl occasionally, 2 minutes. Beat
in egg whites on high speed, scraping bowl
occasionally, 2 minutes. Pour into pans.

Bake until wooden pick inserted in center comes
out clean, 30 to 35 minutes. Cool 10 minutes; remove from pans. Cool completely.

Mocha Butter Frosting

⅓ cup margarine or   1½ teaspoons instant
   butter, softened   powdered coffee
2 ounces melted   1½ teaspoons vanilla
   unsweetened   About 2 tablespoons
   chocolate (cool)   milk
2 cups powdered sugar

Mix margarine and chocolate. Beat in powdered
sugar and coffee. Beat in vanilla and milk until
frosting is smooth and spreading consistency.

Buttercream Frosting

1 cup powdered sugar   ¼ teaspoon almond
2 tablespoons margarine   extract
   or butter, softened   1 tablespoon milk
2 tablespoons shortening

Beat all ingredients on medium speed until frosting is smooth and desired consistency. If necessary,
stir in additional milk, ½ teaspoon at a time.

○ *Time-saver Tip:* Substitute 1 package (18.5
ounces) white cake mix with pudding for the White
Pecan Cake. Prepare and bake as directed on package except stir ½ cup chopped pecans into batter.

Almond Tea Cake

Eggless White Cake   *Almond Fluff (below)*
(below)

Bake Eggless White Cake as directed. Place Almond Fluff in decorating bag with large open star tip #4B. Pipe shell border around base of cake (see page 9). Pass remaining Almond Fluff. Refrigerate any remaining cake. 9 to 12 servings.

Eggless White Cake

2 cups all-purpose flour or 2¼ cups cake flour	½ teaspoon baking soda
	½ teaspoon almond extract
1 cup sugar	⅓ cup sliced almonds
¼ cup shortening, melted	1 tablespoon sugar
1 cup buttermilk	2 tablespoons almond-flavored liqueur
1 teaspoon salt	
½ teaspoon baking powder	

Heat oven to 350°. Grease and flour square pan, 9 × 9 × 2 inches. Beat flour, 1 cup sugar, the shortening, buttermilk, salt, baking powder, baking soda and almond extract in large bowl on medium speed, scraping bowl constantly, until blended, about 30 seconds. Beat on medium speed, scraping bowl occasionally, 3 minutes. Pour into pan; sprinkle with almonds.

Bake until wooden pick inserted in center comes out clean, 30 to 35 minutes. Sprinkle with 1 tablespoon sugar; drizzle with liqueur. Cool 10 minutes; remove from pan. Cool completely.

Almond Fluff

Beat 1 cup chilled whipping cream in chilled bowl until stiff peaks form; fold in 2 tablespoons almond-flavored liqueur.

French Silk Filbert Cake

White Nut Cake (right)   *12 whole filberts*
French Silk Frosting   *1 cup finely chopped*
(right)   *filberts*

Bake White Nut Cake as directed. Reserve ½ cup French Silk Frosting for decorating; fill layers and frost cake with remaining frosting. Mark servings on frosting with serrated knife.

Place reserved frosting in decorating bag with star tip #18. Pipe three-petaled lily onto each serving. Place a whole filbert on each lily. Press chopped filberts into frosting around side. 12 servings.

White Nut Cake

6 egg whites	½ cup margarine or butter, softened
¼ cup sugar	½ cup shortening
2⅔ cups all-purpose flour	4 teaspoons baking powder
1½ cups finely chopped filberts*	1 teaspoon salt
1¼ cups sugar	1 cup milk

Heat oven to 350°. Grease and flour 3 round pans, 8 × 1½ inches. Beat egg whites in large bowl until foamy. Beat in ¼ cup sugar, 1 tablespoon at a time; continue beating until mixture is stiff and glossy. Do not underbeat.

Beat flour, filberts, 1¼ cups sugar, the margarine, shortening, baking powder and salt in another large bowl on medium speed, scraping bowl constantly, until blended, about 30 seconds. Beat in milk on medium speed, scraping bowl occasionally, 2 minutes; fold into egg whites. Pour into pans.

Bake until wooden pick inserted in center comes out clean, 35 to 40 minutes. (Refrigerate 1 layer while 2 are baking.) Cool 10 minutes; remove from pans. Cool completely.

*Finely chopped pecans can be substituted for the finely chopped filberts. Substitute whole pecans for the whole filberts.

French Silk Frosting

4 cups powdered sugar	3 ounces melted unsweetened chocolate (cool)
1 cup margarine or butter, softened	
	1½ teaspoons vanilla
	3 tablespoons milk

Beat all ingredients on medium speed until frosting is smooth and spreading consistency. If necessary, stir in additional milk, 1 teaspoon at a time.

○ *Time-saver Tip:* Substitute 1 package (18.5 ounces) white cake mix with pudding for the White Nut Cake. Prepare and bake as directed on package for two 8-inch rounds except stir ½ cup finely chopped filberts into batter.

Almond Tea Cake, top, French Silk Filbert Cake, bottom

Chocolate-Rum Cream Cake

Chocolate Chip Cake   Rum-Cream Frosting
  (below)   (right)
Dark Chocolate Filling
  (right)

Bake Chocolate Chip Cake as directed. Fill layers to within 1 inch of edge with half of the Dark Chocolate Filling. Spread remaining filling over top of cake. Reserve 1½ cups Rum-Cream Frosting for decorating; frost side of cake with remaining frosting. Place reserved frosting in decorating bag with open star tip #18. Pipe 5 or 6 large rosettes onto top of cake (see page 8). Refrigerate any remaining cake. 12 to 16 servings.

Chocolate Chip Cake

2¼ cups all-purpose   1 teaspoon salt
  flour   1 teaspoon vanilla
1⅔ cups sugar   5 egg whites
 ⅔ cup shortening   ½ cup finely chopped
1¼ cups milk   semisweet chocolate
3½ teaspoons baking   or miniature
  powder   chocolate chips

Heat oven to 350°. Grease and flour 2 round pans, 9 × 1½ inches. Beat flour, sugar, shortening, milk, baking powder, salt and vanilla in large bowl on medium speed, scraping bowl constantly, until blended, about 30 seconds. Beat on high speed, scraping bowl occasionally, 2 minutes. Beat in egg whites on high speed, scraping bowl occasionally, 2 minutes. Stir in chocolate. Pour into pans.

Bake until wooden pick inserted in center comes out clean, 30 to 35 minutes. Cool 10 minutes; remove from pans. Cool completely.

Dark Chocolate Filling

1½ cups sugar   2 squares (1 ounce each)
 ½ cup milk   unsweetened
 2 tablespoons   chocolate, cut up
   margarine or butter   4 egg yolks, beaten

Mix sugar, milk, margarine and chocolate in saucepan. Cook over medium heat, stirring constantly, until margarine and chocolate are melted. Stir at least half of the hot mixture gradually into egg yolks. Blend into hot mixture in saucepan. Heat to boiling, stirring constantly. Boil and stir 2 minutes. Remove from heat; cool without stirring.

Rum-Cream Frosting

Beat 1½ cups chilled whipping cream in chilled bowl until stiff. Fold in 1½ tablespoons rum.

Chocolate-Rum Cream Cake, left, Lemon 'n Spice Marble Cake, right

Lemon 'n Spice Marble Cake

Marble Spice Cake
  (below)

Lemon Butter
  Frosting (right)
1½ teaspoons ground
    allspice

Bake Marble Spice Cake as directed. Reserve 1 cup Lemon Butter Frosting for decorating; fill layers and frost cake with remaining frosting. Stir allspice into reserved frosting; place in decorating bag with open star tip #32. Pipe rope in lattice design across top of cake. Pipe shell border around base and top edge of cake (see page 9). 10 to 14 servings.

Marble Spice Cake

2 cups all-purpose flour	1 teaspoon vanilla
1⅓ cups sugar	3 eggs
½ cup shortening	1 teaspoon ground cinnamon
1 cup milk	
3½ teaspoons baking powder	1 teaspoon ground cloves
1 teaspoon salt	½ teaspoon ground nutmeg

Heat oven to 350°. Grease and flour 2 round pans, 8 × 1½ inches. Beat flour, sugar, shortening, milk, baking powder, salt, vanilla and eggs in large bowl on medium speed, scraping bowl constantly, until blended, about 30 seconds. Beat on medium speed, scraping bowl occasionally, 3 minutes. Mix cinnamon, cloves and nutmeg; stir into ⅓ of the batter. Spoon batters alternately into pans. Cut through batter several times for marbled effect.

Bake until wooden pick inserted in center comes out clean, 35 to 40 minutes. Cool 10 minutes; remove from pans. Cool completely.

Lemon Butter Frosting

4½ cups powdered sugar	1 tablespoon finely shredded lemon peel
3 tablespoons margarine or butter, softened	
	3 tablespoons lemon juice
3 tablespoons shortening	2 tablespoons water

Beat all ingredients on medium speed until frosting is smooth and spreading consistency. If necessary, stir in additional water, 1 teaspoon at a time.

○ *Time-saver Tip:* Substitute 1 package (18.5 ounces) yellow cake mix with pudding for the Marble Spice Cake. Prepare and bake as directed on package except stir 1 teaspoon each ground cinnamon and cloves and ½ teaspoon ground nutmeg into ⅓ of the batter. Spoon batters alternately into pans. Cut through batter several times with spatula for marbled effect.

Neapolitan Patchwork Cake

Neapolitan Patchwork Cake

Marble Cake (right)
Sour Cream Frosting (right)

½ ounce melted semisweet chocolate (cool)
3 drops red food color

Bake Marble Cake as directed. Divide Sour Cream Frosting into 3 parts. Stir chocolate into one part.

Stir food color into one part. Leave one part plain. Mark top of cake into 3-inch squares. Frost squares in alternate colors. Refrigerate any remaining cake. 12 to 15 servings.

Marble Cake

2²/₃ cups all-purpose flour	1 teaspoon salt
1³/₄ cups sugar	2 teaspoons vanilla
¹/₃ cup margarine or butter	5 egg whites
¹/₃ cup shortening	1 ounce melted unsweetened chocolate (cool)
1¹/₄ cups milk	¹/₈ teaspoon red food color
4¹/₂ teaspoons baking powder	

Heat oven to 350°. Grease and flour rectangular pan, 13 × 9 × 2 inches. Beat flour, sugar, margarine, shortening, milk, baking powder, salt and vanilla in large bowl on medium speed, scraping bowl constantly, until blended, about 30 seconds. Beat on high speed, scraping bowl occasionally, 2 minutes. Beat in egg whites on high speed, scraping bowl occasionally, 2 minutes.

Divide batter into 3 parts. Stir chocolate into one part. Stir food color into one part. Leave one part plain. Spoon batters alternately into pan. Cut through batter several times for marbled effect.

Bake until wooden pick inserted in center comes out clean, 40 to 45 minutes. Cool 10 minutes; remove from pan. Cool completely.

Sour Cream Frosting

4 cups powdered sugar	¹/₂ cup dairy sour cream
1 cup all-purpose flour	2 teaspoons vanilla
¹/₂ cup margarine or butter, softened	¹/₂ teaspoon salt
	1 tablespoon water

Beat all ingredients on medium speed until frosting is smooth and spreading consistency. If necessary, stir in additional water, 1 teaspoon at a time.

○ *Time-saver Tip:* Substitute 1 package (18.5 ounces) white cake mix with pudding for the Marble Cake. Prepare and bake as directed on package except divide batter into 3 parts. Stir 1 ounce melted unsweetened chocolate (cool) into one part. Stir ¹/₈ teaspoon red food color into one part. Leave one part plain. Spoon batters alternately into pan. Cut through batter several times with spatula for marbled effect.

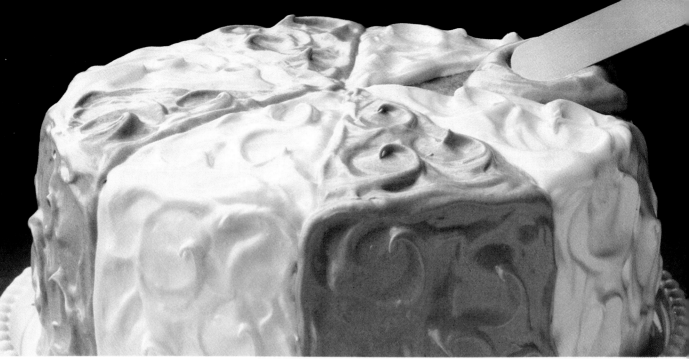

Peppermint Swirl Cake

Peppermint Marble Cake (below)

Peppermint Frosting (right)
5 drops red food color

Bake Peppermint Marble Cake as directed. Fill layers with ¾ cup of the Peppermint Frosting. Stir food color into half of the remaining frosting. Spoon frosting alternately into 8 mounds around the top edge of the cake. Swirl mounds separately down side of cake and across top to center. 12 to 16 servings.

Peppermint Marble Cake

2¼ cups all-purpose flour	1 teaspoon salt
1⅔ cups sugar	1 teaspoon vanilla
⅔ cup shortening	5 egg whites
1¼ cups milk	8 drops red food color
3½ teaspoons baking powder	¼ teaspoon peppermint extract

Heat oven to 350°. Grease and flour 2 round pans, 9 × 1½ inches. Beat flour, sugar, shortening, milk, baking powder, salt and vanilla in large bowl on medium speed, scraping bowl constantly, until blended, about 30 seconds. Beat on high speed, scraping bowl occasionally, 2 minutes. Beat in egg whites on high speed, scraping bowl occasionally, 2 minutes. Stir food color and peppermint extract into ⅓ of the batter. Spoon batters alternately into pans. Cut through batter for marbled effect.

Bake until wooden pick inserted in center comes out clean, 35 to 40 minutes. Cool 10 minutes; remove from pans. Cool completely.

Peppermint Frosting

½ cup sugar	2 egg whites
¼ cup light corn syrup	½ teaspoon peppermint extract
2 tablespoons water	

Mix sugar, corn syrup and water in 1-quart saucepan. Cover and heat to rolling boil over medium heat. Uncover and boil rapidly until candy thermometer registers 242° or until small amount of mixture dropped into very cold water forms a firm ball that holds its shape until pressed.

As mixture boils, beat egg whites in small bowl just until stiff peaks form. Pour hot syrup very slowly in a thin stream into egg whites, beating constantly on medium speed. Add peppermint extract; beat on high speed until stiff peaks form.

○ *Time-saver Tip:* Substitute 1 package (18.5 ounces) white cake mix with pudding for the Peppermint Marble Cake. Prepare and bake as directed on package except stir 8 drops red food color and ¼ teaspoon peppermint extract into ⅓ of the batter. Spoon batters alternately into pans. Cut through batter several times with spatula for marbled effect.

Strawberries and Cream Cake

Whipped Cream Cake (below)
Whipped Cream Cheese Frosting (below)

1 pint strawberries, sliced

Bake Whipped Cream Cake as directed. Spread 1 layer with ½ cup of the Whipped Cream Cheese Frosting; top with layer of sliced strawberries. Place remaining cake layer on top. Spread thin layer of frosting on side of cake.

Place remaining frosting in decorating bag with large open star tip #4B. Pipe vertical rows on side of cake. Pipe shell border around top edge of cake (see page 9). Arrange sliced strawberries on top of cake. Refrigerate remaining cake. 14 to 16 servings.

Whipped Cream Cake

2 cups all-purpose flour or 2¼ cups cake flour
1½ cups sugar
2 teaspoons baking powder

½ teaspoon salt
1½ cups chilled whipping cream
3 eggs
1½ teaspoons vanilla

Heat oven to 350°. Grease and flour 2 round pans, 8 or 9 × 1½ inches. Mix flour, sugar, baking powder and salt. Beat whipping cream in chilled bowl until stiff. Beat eggs in small bowl until very thick and lemon colored, about 5 minutes. Fold eggs and vanilla into whipped cream. Add flour mixture, about ½ cup at a time, folding gently after each addition until blended. Pour into pans.

Bake until wooden pick inserted in center comes out clean, 30 to 35 minutes. Cool 10 minutes; remove from pans. Cool completely.

Whipped Cream Cheese Frosting

1 package (3 ounces) cream cheese, softened
1 tablespoon milk

2 cups chilled whipping cream
⅔ cup powdered sugar

Beat cream cheese and milk in chilled bowl on low speed until smooth; beat in whipping cream and powdered sugar. Beat on high speed, scraping bowl occasionally, until stiff peaks form.

○ *Time-saver Tip:* Substitute 1 package (18.5 ounces) yellow cake mix with pudding for the Whipped Cream Cake. Prepare and bake as directed on package.

Custard-filled Anise Cake

Anise Cake (below)
Custard Cream Filling (below)
Powdered sugar

Strawberries
Green grape clusters
Mint leaves

Bake Anise Cake as directed. Fill layers with Custard Cream Filling. Place paper doily on top layer; press powdered sugar generously through sieve over doily. Carefully remove doily. Garnish base of cake with strawberries, grapes and mint leaves. Refrigerate any remaining cake. 12 to 16 servings.

Anise Cake

2 cups plus 2 tablespoons all-purpose flour
1½ cups sugar
½ cup shortening
1 cup milk

3½ teaspoons baking powder
3 to 4 teaspoons crushed anise seed
1 teaspoon salt
3 eggs

Heat oven to 350°. Grease and flour 2 round pans, 9 × 1½ inches. Beat all ingredients in large bowl on medium speed, scraping bowl constantly, until blended, about 30 seconds. Beat on high speed, scraping bowl occasionally, 3 minutes. Pour batter into pans.

Bake until wooden pick inserted in center comes out clean, 30 to 35 minutes. Cool 10 minutes; remove from pans. Cool completely.

Custard Cream Filling

⅓ cup sugar
¼ tablespoons cornstarch
⅛ teaspoon salt

1½ cups milk
2 egg yolks, slightly beaten
1 teaspoon vanilla

Mix sugar, cornstarch and salt in saucepan. Stir in milk gradually. Cook over medium heat, stirring constantly, until mixture thickens and boils. Boil and stir 1 minute. Stir at least half of the hot mixture gradually into egg yolks. Blend into hot mixture in saucepan. Boil and stir 1 minute. Remove from heat; stir in vanilla. Cool.

○ *Time-saver Tip:* Substitute 1 package (18.5 ounces) yellow cake mix with pudding for the Anise Cake. Prepare and bake as directed on package except add 3 to 4 teaspoons crushed anise seed before beating.

Strawberries and Cream Cake, top,
Custard-filled Anise Cake, bottom

sugar, margarine and water until smooth. If necessary, stir in additional water, a few drops at a time, until desired consistency. Tint frosting orange with 2 or 3 drops yellow and 1 or 2 drops red food color.

Place frosting in decorating bag with writing tip #5. Mark 15 servings on cake. Form a carrot on each serving holding tip at 45° angle close to surface of cake. Starting at narrow end of carrot, gradually increase pressure while slowly moving tip toward you to form carrot. Just before serving, place small sprig of parsley at top of each carrot for green tops. Refrigerate any remaining cake. 15 servings.

Whole Wheat Carrot Cake

1 cup granulated sugar	1 teaspoon baking powder
1 cup packed brown sugar	1 teaspoon salt
1 cup vegetable oil	1 teaspoon ground allspice
1 teaspoon vanilla	1 teaspoon ground cinnamon
4 eggs	
1½ cups whole wheat flour	3 cups finely shredded carrots
½ cup all-purpose flour	1 cup chopped walnuts
1 teaspoon baking soda	

Heat oven to 350°. Grease and flour rectangular pan, 13 × 9 × 2 inches. Stir sugars, oil, vanilla and eggs in large bowl until blended, about 30 seconds; beat 1 minute. Stir in flours, baking soda, baking powder, salt, allspice and cinnamon until blended. Stir in carrots and walnuts. Pour into pan.

Bake until wooden pick inserted in center comes out clean, 45 to 50 minutes. Cool 10 minutes; remove from pan. Cool completely.

Cream Cheese Frosting

1 package (3 ounces) cream cheese, softened	1 teaspoon vanilla
1 tablespoon milk	2½ cups powdered sugar

Mix cream cheese, milk and vanilla. Gradually stir in powdered sugar until smooth and spreading consistency. If necessary, stir in additional milk, ½ teaspoon at a time.

Cream Cheese Carrot Cake

Cream Cheese Carrot Cake

Whole Wheat Carrot Cake (right)	2 tablespoons margarine or butter, softened
Cream Cheese Frosting (right)	1 tablespoon water Yellow and red food color
1 cup powdered sugar	Parsley

Bake Whole Wheat Carrot Cake as directed. Frost cake with Cream Cheese Frosting. Beat powdered

Pecan Cream Torte

Brown Sugar Pecan
Cake (below)
1 cup chilled whipping
cream

2 tablespoons
powdered sugar
Browned Butter
Glaze (below)
12 to 14 pecan halves

Bake Brown Sugar Pecan Cake as directed. Beat whipping cream and powdered sugar in chilled bowl until stiff. Reserve ¾ cup whipped cream for garnish; fill layers with remaining whipped cream. Spread Browned Butter Glaze quickly over top of cake. Cool 5 minutes.

Place reserved whipped cream in decorating bag with large open star tip #4B. Pipe 12 to 14 drop flowers or rosettes around top edge of cake (see page 8). Place pecan halves above each flower. Refrigerate any remaining cake. 12 to 14 servings.

Brown Sugar Pecan Cake

1¾ cups all-purpose
flour
1½ cups packed brown
sugar
¾ cup margarine or
butter, softened
1 cup milk

2 teaspoons baking
powder
¼ teaspoon salt
1½ teaspoons vanilla
3 eggs
1 cup finely chopped
pecans

Heat oven to 350°. Grease and flour 3 round pans, 8 × 1½ inches. Beat all ingredients except pecans in large bowl on medium speed, scraping bowl constantly, until blended, about 30 seconds. Beat on high speed, scraping bowl occasionally, 3 minutes. Stir in pecans. Pour into pans. (⅓ of the batter [about 1⅔ cups] can be refrigerated while 2 layers are baking.)

Bake until wooden pick inserted in center comes out clean, 20 to 25 minutes. Cool 10 minutes; remove from pans. Cool completely.

Browned Butter Glaze

2 tablespoons margarine
or butter
1 cup powdered sugar

1 teaspoon vanilla
1 tablespoon hot water

Heat margarine in saucepan over medium heat until delicate brown. Cool slightly. Stir in powdered sugar, vanilla and water. If necessary, stir in additional hot water, 1 teaspoon at a time, until glaze is desired consistency.

Marzipan Torte

Golden Pound Cake
  (right)
1 jar (12 ounces)
  apricot preserves
1 package (7 ounces)
  marzipan

½ cup sliced almonds
½ cup powdered sugar
2 teaspoons water
2 teaspoons cocoa
  Red food color

Bake Golden Pound Cake as directed. Split cake to make 4 layers (see page 12). If necessary, break up any large pieces of apricot in preserves. Fill each layer with scant ¼ cup of the apricot preserves. Brush side and top of cake lightly with preserves.

Reserve half of the marzipan for top of cake. Shape half of the remaining marzipan into rectangle, about 4 × 1 inch. Place between waxed paper; roll with rolling pin into rectangle, 12 × 3 inches (it will be very thin). Trim sides to make even, pressing trimmings on ends if necessary for the 12 × 3-inch rectangle.

Lift waxed paper off top of marzipan. Using remaining waxed paper to facilitate transfer, lift marzipan and waxed paper together as shown in diagram and carefully press marizpan onto half of cake side (press any excess over top edge of cake). Remove waxed paper. Repeat with remaining fourth of marzipan. Smooth edges together with spatula to join.

Add any remaining marzipan trimmings to reserved half of marzipan; shape into flattened round. Roll between waxed paper into 8-inch circle. Lift waxed paper off top of marzipan. Lift remaining waxed paper and marzipan together, invert and press onto top of cake. Press to join marzipan around top edge of cake. Carefully remove waxed paper. Brush side only of cake lightly with apricot preserves; press almonds into marzipan to coat side of cake.

Mix powdered sugar and water; reserve 1 tablespoon of the frosting for flowers. Stir cocoa and enough additional water, a few drops at a time until desired consistency, into remaining frosting. Place in small sturdy plastic storage bag; cut off very small corner of bag to make writing tip. Draw desired design lightly in marzipan with wooden pick. Fold over top of bag; press out frosting to follow design.

Stir 3 or 4 drops red food color into reserved frosting. Place in another small sturdy plastic storage bag; pipe 3 to 5 small dots to form each flower. 16 servings.

NOTE: Keep marzipan covered at all times to prevent drying. If marzipan sticks, sprinkle hands lightly with powdered sugar. Marzipan can be rerolled easily if necessary. When rolling marzipan for sides of cake, lift rolling pin slightly at ends of marzipan to prevent ends from becoming too thin. When rolling marzipan for top, roll from center to outside evenly in all directions.

Golden Pound Cake

2 cups all-purpose flour
1 cup sugar
¼ cup margarine or
  butter, softened
¼ cup shortening
¾ cup milk
2 eggs

3 teaspoons baking
  powder
1 teaspoon salt
1 teaspoon almond
  extract
1 teaspoon vanilla

Heat oven to 350°. Grease and flour 2 round pans, 8 × 1½ inches. Beat all ingredients in large bowl on medium speed, scraping bowl constantly, until blended, about 30 seconds. Beat on high speed, scraping bowl occasionally, 3 minutes.

Bake until wooden pick inserted in center comes out clean, 30 to 35 minutes. Cool 10 minutes; remove from pans. Cool completely.

○ Time-saver Tip: Substitute 1 package (16 ounces) golden pound cake mix for the Golden Pound Cake. Prepare as directed on package except add 1 teaspoon almond extract before beating. Bake in 2 round pans, 8 × 1½ inches, 30 to 35 minutes.

Placing Marzipan on Marzipan Cake

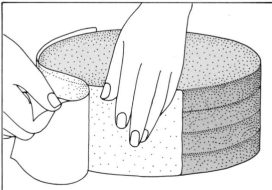

Lift marzipan and waxed paper together; press marzipan onto half of cake side. Remove wax paper. Repeat with remaining side.

Clockwise from top: Marzipan Torte, Graham Cracker Cream Torte (page 138), Mocha Cream Torte (page 138)

Graham Cracker Cream Torte

Graham Cracker Cake (below)	⅓ cup packed brown sugar
1½ cups chilled whipping cream	1 teaspoon vanilla
	14 to 16 walnut halves

Bake Graham Cracker Cake as directed. Beat whipping cream, brown sugar and vanilla in chilled bowl until stiff. Reserve 1¼ cups whipped cream for decorating. Fill layers and frost cake with remaining whipped cream.

Place reserved whipped cream in decorating bag with open star tip #32. Pipe loops onto each serving as shown; garnish each serving with walnut half. 14 to 16 servings.

Graham Cracker Cake

3 eggs, separated	1 cup milk
1 cup packed brown sugar	3 teaspoons baking powder
2 cups graham cracker crumbs (about 24 squares)	¼ teaspoon salt
	1 teaspoon vanilla
⅔ cup all-purpose flour	½ cup finely chopped nuts
⅓ cup margarine or butter, softened	

Heat oven to 350°. Grease and flour 2 round pans, 9 × 1½ inches. Beat egg whites in small bowl on high speed until foamy. Beat in ½ cup of the brown sugar, 1 tablespoon at a time; beat until very thick and glossy. Do not underbeat. Transfer mixture to large bowl.

Beat remaining brown sugar, the cracker crumbs, flour, margarine, milk, baking powder, salt, vanilla and egg yolks in another large bowl on medium speed, scraping bowl constantly, until blended, about 30 seconds. Beat on high speed, scraping bowl occasionally, 2 minutes. Fold batter and nuts into egg white mixture. Pour into pans.

Bake until wooden pick inserted in center comes out clean, 30 to 35 minutes. Cool 10 minutes; remove from pans. Cool completely.

Mocha Cream Torte

Golden Pound Loaf (below)	Brazil Nut Curls (below) and chocolate coffee beans
Mocha Cream Frosting (below)	

Bake Golden Pound Loaf as directed. Freeze cooled cake uncovered until firm, about 1½ hours. Cut cake horizontally into 5 layers. Spread scant ¼ cup Mocha Cream Frosting between each layer; frost sides and top of cake with remaining frosting.

Mark diagonal lines with tines of fork across top and down sides of cake. Garnish with Brazil Nut Curls and coffee beans. 14 to 16 servings.

Golden Pound Loaf

2 cups all-purpose flour	3 teaspoons baking powder
1 cup sugar	1 teaspoon salt
¼ cup margarine or butter, softened	1 teaspoon vanilla
¼ cup shortening	2 eggs
¾ cup milk	

Heat oven to 350°. Grease and flour loaf pan, 9 × 5 × 3 inches. Beat all ingredients in large bowl on medium speed, scraping bowl constantly, until blended, about 30 seconds. Beat on high speed, scraping bowl occasionally, 3 minutes. Pour batter into pan.

Bake until wooden pick inserted in center comes out clean, 60 to 65 minutes. Cool 10 minutes; remove from pan. Cool completely.

Mocha Cream Frosting

1 tablespoon instant coffee	¾ cup margarine or butter, softened
2 tablespoons hot water	1 tablespoon cocoa
4 cups powdered sugar	1 teaspoon water

Dissolve instant coffee in hot water. Beat coffee and remaining ingredients on medium speed until smooth and spreading consistency. If necessary, stir in additional water, ½ teaspoon at a time.

Brazil Nut Curls

Cut thin lengthwise slices from Brazil nuts with a vegetable parer.

○ *Time-saver Tip:* Substitute 1 package (16 ounces) golden pound cake mix for the Golden Pound Loaf. Prepare and bake as directed on package.

Apricot-glazed Pound Cake

Apricot Brandy
  Pound Cake (below)
1/2 cup apricot preserves
1 tablespoon apricot
  brandy or apricot
  nectar

1 can (about 8³/4
  ounces) apricot
  halves, drained
Mint leaves
1 cup dairy sour cream
1/4 cup packed brown
  sugar

Bake Apricot Brandy Pound Cake as directed. Heat apricot preserves until melted; remove from heat. Cut up any large pieces of fruit. Stir in apricot brandy. Spread warm apricot glaze over cake. Garnish with apricot halves and mint leaves. Mix sour cream and brown sugar. Serve sweetened sour cream and any remaining apricot halves with cake. 16 servings.

Apricot Brandy Pound Cake

3 cups all-purpose flour
3 cups sugar
1 cup margarine or
  butter, softened
1 cup dairy sour cream
1/2 cup apricot brandy or
  apricot nectar
1/2 teaspoon salt

1/4 teaspoon baking soda
1 teaspoon orange
  extract
1 teaspoon lemon extract
1 teaspoon almond
  extract
6 eggs

Heat oven to 325°. Grease and flour 12-cup bundt cake pan or tube pan, 10 × 4 inches. Beat all ingredients in large bowl on medium speed, scraping bowl constantly, until blended, about 30 seconds. Beat on high speed, scraping bowl occasionally, 2 minutes. Pour into pan.

Bake until wooden pick inserted in center comes out clean, 1 hour 10 minutes to 1 hour 20 minutes. Cool 20 minutes; remove from pan. Cool cake completely.

Brown Sugar Cream Cake

Brown Sugar Pound
  Cake (below)
2 cups chilled whipping
  cream

1/2 cup packed brown
  sugar
1 teaspoon ground
  ginger
Pecan halves

Bake Brown Sugar Pound Cake as directed. Beat whipping cream, brown sugar and ginger in chilled bowl until stiff. Frost top of cake. Place whipped cream in decorating bag with large open star tip #4B. Pipe whipped cream stars onto inner and outer rims of top and around side of cake (see page 8). Fill center ring with pecan halves and, if desired, serve with sliced fresh or frozen peaches or strawberries. 16 to 20 servings.

Brown Sugar Pound Cake

2¼ cups packed brown
  sugar
1/2 cup granulated
  sugar
3/4 cup margarine or
  butter, softened
1/2 cup shortening
1½ teaspoons vanilla
5 eggs

3 cups all-purpose
  flour or 3¹/3 cups
  cake flour
1½ teaspoons baking
  powder
1/2 teaspoon salt
1 cup milk
1 cup chopped pecans

Heat oven to 325°. Grease and flour tube pan, 10 × 4 inches. Beat sugars, margarine, shortening, vanilla and eggs in large bowl on medium speed, scraping bowl constantly, until blended, about 30 seconds. Beat on high speed, scraping bowl occasionally, 2 minutes. Beat in flour, baking powder and salt alternately with milk on low speed. Stir in pecans. Pour into pan.

Bake until wooden pick inserted in center comes out clean, 1 hour 20 minutes to 1 hour 30 minutes. Cool 20 minutes; remove from pan. Cool cake completely.

TWO QUICK DECORATING TRICKS

Draw a design on frosted cake or use cookie cutter dipped in food color and pressed into frosting. Fill in design with crushed candies, colored sugar or chopped nuts.

For a plaid design, frost cake with a fluffy frosting. Dip a piece of white sewing thread in liquid food color; stretching it taut, press into frosting. Repeat, using new thread for each color.

Chocolate Sundae Cake

Chocolate Syrup Cake (below)
Chocolate Sundae Frosting (below)

1 to 2 tablespoons chocolate syrup

Bake Chocolate Syrup Cake as directed. Fill layers and frost cake with Chocolate Sundae Frosting. Drizzle chocolate syrup over top of cake and around top edge, letting it run down side unevenly. Refrigerate any remaining cake. 12 to 16 servings.

Chocolate Syrup Cake

2¹⁄₃ cups all-purpose flour
1¹⁄₂ cups sugar
¹⁄₂ cup shortening
³⁄₄ cup buttermilk
¹⁄₂ cup water
¹⁄₂ cup chocolate syrup

1 teaspoon baking soda
1 teaspoon salt
¹⁄₂ teaspoon baking powder
1 teaspoon vanilla
2 eggs
¹⁄₂ cup chocolate syrup

Heat oven to 350°. Grease and flour 2 round pans, 9 × 1¹⁄₂ inches. Beat all ingredients except ¹⁄₂ cup chocolate syrup in large bowl on medium speed, scraping bowl constantly, until blended, about 30 seconds. Beat on medium speed, scraping bowl occasionally, 3 minutes.

Reserve ¹⁄₂ cup chocolate batter; pour remaining batter into pans. Stir remaining ¹⁄₂ cup chocolate syrup into reserved batter. Pour half of the mixture over batter in each pan. Cut through batter several times for marbled effect.

Bake until wooden pick inserted in center comes out clean, about 35 minutes. Cool 10 minutes; remove from pans. Cool completely.

Chocolate Sundae Frosting

Beat 1 cup chilled whipping cream and ¹⁄₄ cup chocolate syrup in chilled bowl until stiff.

Yardstick for Yields

Size and Kind	Servings
8-inch layer cake	10 to 14
9-inch layer	12 to 16
13 × 9 × 2-inch rectangular cake	12 to 15
8- or 9-inch square cake	9
angel or chiffon cake	12 to 16

Chocolate Spiral Peanut Butter Cake

Peanut Butter Chiffon Layer Cake (below)
Peanut Butter Frosting (below)

¹⁄₃ cup chopped salted peanuts
1 ounce melted unsweetened chocolate (cool)

Bake Peanut Butter Chiffon Layer Cake as directed. Remove from pans. Fill layers with 1 cup Peanut Butter Frosting; frost cake with remaining frosting. Hold a flexible spatula at the center of the top of the cake; draw the spatula very slowly toward you, rotating cake plate as you do so. Sprinkle spiral with peanuts; outline with chocolate. 10 to 14 servings.

Peanut Butter Chiffon Layer Cake

2 eggs, separated
¹⁄₂ cup granulated sugar
2 cups all-purpose flour
3 teaspoons baking powder
1 teaspoon salt

¹⁄₄ teaspoon baking soda
1 cup packed brown sugar
¹⁄₃ cup chunk-style peanut butter
¹⁄₃ cup vegetable oil
1¹⁄₄ cups milk

Heat oven to 350°. Grease and flour 2 round pans, 8 or 9 × 1¹⁄₂ inches. Beat egg whites on medium speed until foamy. Beat in granulated sugar on high speed, 1 tablespoon at a time; continue beating until stiff and glossy. Do not underbeat.

Mix flour, baking powder, salt and baking soda in large bowl. Add brown sugar, peanut butter, oil and half of the milk. Beat on low speed until moistened. Beat on high speed, scraping bowl constantly, 1 minute. Add remaining milk and the egg yolks. Beat on high speed, scraping bowl occasionally, 1 minute. Fold in meringue. Pour batter into pans.

Bake until wooden pick inserted in center comes out clean, 30 to 35 minutes. Cool completely.

Peanut Butter Frosting

4 cups powdered sugar
¹⁄₂ cup creamy peanut butter

¹⁄₄ cup shortening
¹⁄₃ cup milk

Beat all ingredients on medium speed until frosting is smooth and spreading consistency. If necessary, stir in additional milk, 1 teaspoon at a time.

Clockwise from top: Chocolate Sundae Cake, Brown Sugar Cream Cake (page 139), Chocolate Spiral Peanut Butter Cake

Banana-Nutmeg Cream Cake

Banana Chiffon Layer
  Cake (below)
Nutmeg Whipped Cream
  (right)

Chocolate-dipped Banana
  Slices (right)

Bake Banana Chiffon Layer Cake as directed. Remove from pans. Reserve 2½ cups Nutmeg Whipped Cream for decorating; fill layers and frost cake with remaining whipped cream mixture.

Place reserved whipped cream in decorating bag with large open star tip #4B. Pipe reverse shell border around base of cake (see page 9). Decorate top of cake with Chocolate-dipped Banana Slices. Refrigerate any remaining cake. 10 to 14 servings.

Banana Chiffon Layer Cake

2 eggs, separated
1⅓ cups sugar
1¾ cups all-purpose
     flour
1 teaspoon baking
     powder
1 teaspoon baking soda
1 teaspoon salt

1 cup mashed bananas
     (2 to 3 medium)
⅔ cup buttermilk
⅓ cup vegetable oil
1 teaspoon vanilla
½ cup finely chopped
     walnuts

Heat oven to 350°. Grease and flour 2 round pans, 8 or 9 × 1½ inches. Beat egg whites on medium speed until foamy. Beat in ⅓ cup of the sugar on high speed, 1 tablespoon at a time; continue beating until stiff and glossy. Do not underbeat.

Mix remaining sugar, the flour, baking powder, baking soda and salt in large bowl. Add bananas, half of the buttermilk, the oil and vanilla. Beat on medium speed until moistened. Beat on high speed, scraping bowl constantly, 1 minute. Add remaining buttermilk and the egg yolks. Beat on high speed, scraping bowl occasionaly, 1 minute. Fold in meringue and walnuts. Pour into pans.

Bake until wooden pick inserted in center comes out clean, 30 to 35 minutes. Cool completely.

Nutmeg Whipped Cream

Beat 3 cups chilled whipping cream, 1 cup powdered sugar and 1½ teaspoons ground nutmeg in chilled bowl until stiff.

Chocolate-dipped Banana Slices

1 medium banana
     Lemon juice
½ cup semisweet
     chocolate chips

1 teaspoon margarine or
     butter

Cut banana diagonally into ¼-inch slices. Dip slices into lemon juice; drain. Heat chocolate chips and margarine over low heat, stirring constantly, until chocolate is melted. Cool slightly. Dip half of each banana slice into chocolate mixture; place on waxed paper. Let stand until set.

Banana-Nutmeg Cream Cake

Caramel Spice Cake

Caramel Spice Cake

Sour Cream Spice Cake (below) *Caramel Fluffy Frosting (right)*

Bake Sour Cream Spice Cake as directed. Prepare Caramel Fluffy Frosting. Reserve 2 cups of the frosting for decorating; fill layers and frost cake with remaining frosting.

Place reserved frosting in decorating bag with large open star tip #4B. Pipe a reverse scroll on side of cake. Pipe a rosette (see page 8) on each serving on top of cake. 12 to 16 servings.

Sour Cream Spice Cake

2 cups all-purpose flour	1¼ teaspoons baking soda
1½ cups packed brown sugar	1 teaspoon baking powder
¼ cup margarine or butter, softened	¾ teaspoon ground cloves
¼ cup shortening	½ teaspoon salt
1 cup dairy sour cream	½ teaspoon ground nutmeg
½ cup water	2 eggs
2 teaspoons ground cinnamon	1 cup raisins, cut up
	½ cup chopped walnuts

Heat oven to 350°. Grease and flour 2 round pans, 8 or 9 × 1½ inches. Beat all ingredients except raisins and walnuts in large bowl on medium speed, scraping bowl constantly, until blended, about 30 seconds. Beat on high speed, scraping bowl occasionally, 3 minutes. Fold in raisins and walnuts. Pour into pans.

Bake until wooden pick inserted in center comes out clean, 40 to 45 minutes. Cool 10 minutes; remove from pans. Cool completely.

NOTE: Cake can also be baked in rectangular pan, 13 × 9 × 2 inches, 40 to 45 minutes.

Caramel Fluffy Frosting

¾ cup packed brown sugar	3 tablespoons water
⅓ cup light corn syrup	3 egg whites
	½ teaspoon vanilla

Mix brown sugar, corn syrup and water in 1-quart saucepan. Cover and heat to rolling boil over medium heat. Uncover and boil rapidly until candy thermometer registers 242° or until small amount of mixture dropped into very cold water forms a firm ball that holds its shape until pressed.

As mixture boils, beat egg whites in small bowl just until stiff peaks form. Pour hot syrup very slowly in a thin stream into egg whites, beating constantly on medium speed. Add vanilla; beat on high speed until stiff peaks form.

○ *Time-saver Tip:* Substitute 1 package (18.5 ounces) yellow cake mix with pudding for the Sour Cream Spice Cake. Prepare and bake as directed on package except add 2 teaspoons ground cinnamon, ¾ teaspoon ground cloves and ½ teaspoon ground nutmeg before beating. Fold 1 cup raisins, cut up, and ½ cup chopped walnuts into batter.

Butterscotch Sundae Cake

*Butterscotch Cake
(below)*
*White Mountain
Frosting (page 16)*

*3 tablespoons margarine
or butter*
*¼ cup packed brown
sugar*
2 tablespoons water

Bake Butterscotch Cake as directed. Fill layers and frost cake with White Mountain Frosting. Heat margarine in small saucepan until melted. Stir in brown sugar and water. Heat to boiling, stirring constantly, boil 1½ minutes; remove from heat.

Make petal outline on top of cake with spatula; fill in outline with butterscotch sauce. Drizzle remaining sauce around top edge of cake, letting it run down side unevenly. Top with maraschino cherry if desired. 12 to 16 servings.

Butterscotch Cake

*2¼ cups all-purpose
flour*
*1¾ cups packed brown
sugar*
½ cup shortening
1 cup milk

*3 teaspoons baking
powder*
1 teaspoon salt
1 teaspoon vanilla
2 eggs

Heat oven to 350°. Grease and flour 2 round pans, 9 × 1½ inches. Beat all ingredients in large bowl on medium speed, scraping bowl constantly, until blended, about 30 seconds. Beat on high speed, scraping bowl occasionally, 3 minutes. Pour batter into pans.

Bake until wooden pick inserted in center comes out clean, 30 to 35 minutes. Cool 10 minutes; remove from pans. Cool completely.

○ *Time-saver Tip:* Substitute 1 package (18.5 ounces) yellow cake mix with pudding for the Butterscotch Cake. Prepare and bake as directed on package. Substitute 1 package (7.2 ounces) fluffy white frosting mix for the White Mountain Frosting. Prepare as directed on package.

Butterscotch Sundae Cake, top, Maple-Pecan Cake, bottom

Maple-Pecan Cake

*Maple Buttermilk Cake
(below)*
*Maple Butter Frosting
(below)*

*1 cup finely chopped
pecans*

Bake Maple Buttermilk Cake as directed. Fill layers and frost side only of cake with Maple Butter Frosting. Place pecans on waxed paper. Hold cake as shown in diagram; roll side carefully in pecans to coat. Frost top of cake with remaining frosting in spiral design with large spatula. 14 to 16 servings.

Maple-Buttermilk Cake

*2½ cups all-purpose
flour or 2¾ cups
cake flour*
1½ cups sugar
*½ cup margarine or
butter, softened*
¼ cup shortening

1½ cups buttermilk
*1½ teaspoons baking
soda*
¾ teaspoon salt
*1½ teaspoons maple
flavoring*
3 eggs

Heat oven to 350°. Grease and flour two 9-inch or three 8-inch round pans. Beat all ingredients in large bowl on medium speed, scraping bowl constantly, until blended, about 30 seconds. Beat on high speed, scraping bowl occasionally, 3 minutes. Pour into pans.

Bake until wooden pick inserted in center comes out clean, 30 to 35 minutes. Cool 10 minutes; remove from pans. Cool completely.

Maple Butter Frosting

Mix 3 cups powdered sugar, ⅓ cup margarine or butter, softened, and ⅓ cup maple-flavored syrup; beat until frosting is smooth and spreading consistency. If necessary, stir in additional syrup, ½ teaspoon at a time.

Rolling Cake in Chopped Pecans

Holding filled layers between palms of hands, carefully roll frosted side in chopped pecans to coat.

Peach Melba Cake

Whole Wheat Caramel
Cake (below)
1 cup boiling water
1 package (3 ounces)
raspberry-flavored
gelatin

¾ cup cold water
3 or 4 peaches
1½ cups chilled
whipping cream
3 tablespoons sugar
1 teaspoon vanilla

Bake Whole Wheat Caramel Cake as directed.
Pour boiling water on gelatin in bowl; stir until
gelatin is dissolved. Stir in cold water. Reserve ¼
cup of the gelatin mixture for glaze; refrigerate
remaining gelatin mixture until it mounds slightly
when dropped from a spoon, 1 to 2 hours.

Finely chop enough peaches to measure 1½ cups;
stir into partially set gelatin. Refrigerate until
almost set, about 30 minutes. Refrigerate reserved
gelatin until syrupy, about 20 minutes. Split cake to
make 4 layers (see page 12). Spread 3 layers with ⅓
of the peach gelatin mixture each. Top with remaining layer. Thinly slice remaining peaches;
arrange on top of cake. Brush or spoon reserved
gelatin over peaches.

Beat whipping cream, sugar and vanilla in chilled
bowl until stiff. Reserve 2 cups for decorating.
Spread smooth layer of whipped cream on sides of
torte. Place reserved whipped cream in decorating
bag with large open star tip #4B. Pipe shell border
around base and top edge of cake (see page 9).
Refrigerate any remaining cake. 12 to 15 servings.

Whole Wheat Caramel Cake

1 cup whole wheat flour
1 cup all-purpose flour
1 cup packed brown
sugar
¼ cup granulated sugar
½ cup shortening (half
margarine or butter,
softened, if desired)

1 cup milk
3½ teaspoons baking
powder
1 teaspoon salt
3 eggs

Heat oven to 350°. Grease and flour 2 square pans,
8×8×2 inches, or 2 round pans, 8 or 9×1½ inches. Beat all ingredients in large bowl on medium
speed, scraping bowl constantly, until blended,
about 30 seconds. Beat on high speed, scraping
bowl occasionally, 3 minutes. Pour into pans.

Bake until wooden pick inserted in center comes
out clean, 30 to 35 minutes. Cool 10 minutes; remove from pans. Cool completely.

Lemon-Grape Cake

Lemon Cake (below)
Lemon Cream
Frosting (below)
½ cup chopped green
grapes, well drained

8 to 10 green grapes
Lemon Cup (below), if
desired

Bake Lemon Cake as directed. Prepare Lemon
Cream Frosting; fold chopped grapes into ½ cup
of the frosting. Split cake to make 4 layers (see page
12). Fill and frost cake with Lemon Cream Frosting,
using grape mixture for middle layer.

Cut grapes into fourths; decorate top of cake. Place
Lemon Cup in center. Clusters of grapes can be
placed around base of cake if desired. Refrigerate
any remaining cake. 12 to 16 servings.

Lemon Cake

2 cups all-purpose
flour
1½ cups sugar
½ cup shortening
1 cup milk
3½ teaspoons baking
powder

1 tablespoon finely
shredded lemon peel
1 teaspoon salt
1 teaspoon vanilla
3 eggs

Heat oven to 350°. Grease and flour 2 round pans,
8 or 9×1½ inches. Beat all ingredients in large
bowl on medium speed, scraping bowl constantly,
until blended, about 30 seconds. Beat on high
speed, scraping bowl occasionally, 3 minutes. Pour
into pans.

Bake until wooden pick inserted in center comes
out clean, 30 to 35 minutes. Cool 10 minutes; remove from pans. Cool completely.

Lemon Cream Frosting

1 package (3¼
ounces) lemon
pudding and pie
filling

1 tablespoon finely
shredded lemon peel
1 cup chilled whipping
cream

Prepare pudding and pie filling as directed on
package. Stir in lemon peel; cool. Beat whipping
cream in chilled bowl until stiff; fold in pudding.

Lemon Cup

Cut top off lemon; scoop out inside. Snip top edge
in zigzag fashion to resemble tulip. Just before
serving, place 4 to 6 sugar cubes, which have been
soaked in lemon extract, in lemon cup; ignite.

*Clockwise from top: Peach Melba Cake, Lemon-Grape Cake,
Lemon Prune Cake (page 148)*

Lemon Prune Cake

Prune Spice Cake (below)
Lemon Swirl
  Frosting (page 105)

Lemon slices
Walnut halves
  Pitted uncooked prunes

Bake Prune Spice Cake as directed. Frost cake with Lemon Swirl Frosting. Cut lemon slices into fourths; decorate alternate servings of cake with lemon pieces and walnut halves. Decorate remaining servings with cut-up prunes. Refrigerate any remaining cake. 15 servings.

Prune Spice Cake

1 cup boiling water	1 teaspoon salt
1 cup cut-up pitted uncooked prunes	1 teaspoon ground cinnamon
2 cups all-purpose flour	1 teaspoon ground cloves
1½ cups sugar	1 teaspoon ground nutmeg
½ cup vegetable oil	1 teaspoon vanilla
1¼ teaspoons baking soda	3 eggs
	1 cup chopped walnuts

Pour boiling water on prunes in large bowl; let stand 1 hour. Heat oven to 350°. Grease and flour rectangular pan, 13 × 9 × 2 inches. Beat prunes and remaining ingredients on medium speed, scraping bowl constantly, until blended, about 1 minute. Beat on medium speed, scraping bowl occasionally, 2 minutes. Pour into pan.

Bake until wooden pick inserted in center comes out clean, 45 to 50 minutes. Cool 10 minutes; remove from pan. Cool completely.

Rhubarb-Butterscotch Meringue Cake

Rhubarb Spice Cake
  (right)
Butterscotch Meringue
  (right)

Rhubarb Filling (right),
  if desired

Bake Rhubarb Spice Cake as directed. Place cake on ungreased cookie sheet. Heat oven to 400°. Place Butterscotch Meringue in decorating bag with large open star tip #8. Pipe crisscross design across cake to within ½ inch of edge; pipe meringue around top of cake about ¼ inch from edge.

Bake until meringue is light brown, 8 to 10 minutes. Just before serving, spoon Rhubarb Filling within meringue diamonds. 15 servings.

Rhubarb Spice Cake

⅓ cup boiling water	1 teaspoon salt
2 cups frozen cut rhubarb, rinsed, drained and chopped*	1 teaspoon ground cinnamon
2 cups all-purpose flour	1 teaspoon ground nutmeg
1¼ cups sugar	1 teaspoon ground cloves
½ cup vegetable oil	1 teaspoon vanilla
1¼ teaspoons baking soda	3 eggs
	1 cup chopped nuts

Heat oven to 350°. Pour boiling water over rhubarb in large bowl. Grease and flour rectangular pan, 13 × 9 × 2 inches. Beat rhubarb with liquid and remaining ingredients on medium speed, scraping bowl constantly, until blended, about 1 minute. Beat on medium speed, scraping bowl occasionally, 2 minutes. Pour into pan.

Bake until wooden pick inserted in center comes out clean, 45 to 50 minutes. Cool 10 minutes; remove from pan.

*Half of a 16-ounce package frozen cut rhubarb yields 2 cups; 1¾ cups finely chopped fresh rhubarb can be substituted for the frozen rhubarb.

Butterscotch Meringue

Beat 3 egg whites and ¼ teaspoon cream of tartar until foamy. Beat in ¾ cup packed brown sugar, 1 tablespoon at a time; continue beating until stiff and glossy. Do not underbeat.

Rhubarb Filling

Heat ½ cup sugar and ¼ cup water to boiling, stirring occasionally; reduce heat. Add 2 cups fresh or frozen cut rhubarb (½-inch pieces). Simmer uncovered until rhubarb is tender and slightly transparent, 8 to 10 minutes. Stir in few drops red food color if desired. Cool.

Clockwise from top: Browned Butter Applesauce Cupcakes (page 150), Chocolate Cream Cones (page 150), Chocolate Daisy Cupcakes

Chocolate Daisy Cupcakes

Quick Cocoa Cupcakes (below)

Creamy White Frosting (right)

Chocolate Daisies (right)

Bake Quick Cocoa Cupcakes as directed. Frost with Creamy White Frosting, making top smooth. Place a Chocolate Daisy on each cupcake. 12 cupcakes.

Quick Cocoa Cupcakes

1²/₃ cups all-purpose flour	¹/₂ teaspoon salt
1 cup packed brown sugar	1 cup water
	¹/₃ cup vegetable oil
¹/₄ cup cocoa	1 teaspoon vinegar
1 teaspoon baking soda	¹/₂ teaspoon vanilla

Heat oven to 350°. Mix flour, brown sugar, cocoa, baking soda and salt with fork or spoon. Stir in remaining ingredients until completely mixed. Pour into paper-lined medium muffin cups, 2¹/₂ × 1¹/₄ inches, filling each about ²/₃ full.

Bake until wooden pick inserted in center comes out clean, about 20 minutes. Immediately remove from pan; cool completely.

NOTE: Recipe can be doubled.

Creamy White Frosting

2 cups powdered sugar	1 tablespoon milk
¹/₄ cup margarine or butter, softened	

Beat all ingredients until frosting is smooth and spreading consistency. If necessary, stir in additional milk, ¹/₄ teaspoon at a time.

Chocolate Daisies

Heat ¹/₃ cup semisweet chocolate chips in saucepan over low heat, stirring occasionally, until melted. Place chocolate in small sturdy plastic storage bag or decorating bag with small writing tip. Cut off very small corner of bag, about ¹/₈-inch in diameter. Pipe chocolate in daisy design onto waxed paper-lined cookie sheet. Refrigerate until set, about 30 minutes. Place on frosted cupcakes. 12 daisies.

NOTE: Other designs can be substituted for the daisies such as initials, butterflies, spirals or bows. The design can be drawn on paper and placed under the waxed paper to use as a guide as shown in the photograph. Or the design can be piped directly onto the frosted cupcake if desired.

Chocolate Cream Cones

Chocolate Cupcakes (below)

Chocolate Cream (below)

18 chocolate candy kisses

Bake Chocolate Cupcakes as directed. Place Chocolate Cream in decorating bag with large open star tip #4B. Pipe in a spiral cone shape onto cupcakes. Tp each with candy kiss. Refrigerate any remaining cupcakes. 1½ dozen cupcakes.

Chocolate Cupcakes

1⅓ cups sugar	1¼ teaspoons baking powder
1¼ cups all-purpose flour	½ teaspoon salt
3 tablespoons shortening	¼ teaspoon baking soda
1 cup milk	½ teaspoon vanilla
3 ounces melted unsweetened chocolate (cool)	1 egg

Heat oven to 350°. Beat all ingredients in large bowl on medium speed, scraping bowl constantly, until blended, about 30 seconds. Beat on high speed, scraping bowl occasionally, 3 minutes. Pour into paper-lined medium muffin cups, 2½ × 1¼ inches, filling each ⅔ full.

Bake until wooden pick inserted in center comes out clean, 20 to 25 minutes. Immediately remove from pan; cool completely.

Chocolate Cream

Beat 3 cups chilled whipping cream, 1½ cups powdered sugar and ¾ cup cocoa in chilled bowl until stiff peaks form.

NOTE: Chocolate Cupcakes can be baked in waffle ice cream cones. Fill each ½ full and place on a cookie sheet. Bake as directed.

○ *Time-saver Tip:* Substitute 1 package (18.5 ounces) devils food cake mix with pudding for the Chocolate Cupcakes. Prepare and bake as directed on package for cupcakes.

Browned Butter Applesauce Cupcakes

Applesauce Cupcakes (below)

Browned Butter Frosting (below)

12 semisweet chocolate chips

Sliced almonds

Bake Applesauce Cupcakes as directed. Frost with Browned Butter Frosting. Place a chocolate chip in center of each cupcake; arrange almond slices around chocolate chips to resemble petals of a flower. 1 dozen cupcakes.

Applesauce Cupcakes

1⅔ cups all-purpose flour	½ teaspoon salt
1 cup packed brown sugar	½ cup applesauce
	½ cup water
1½ teaspoons allspice	⅓ cup vegetable oil
1 teaspoon baking soda	1 teaspoon vinegar

Heat oven to 350°. Mix flour, brown sugar, allspice, baking soda and salt with spoon. Stir in remaining ingredients until completely mixed. Pour into paper-lined medium muffin cups, 2½ × 1¼ inches, filling each about ⅔ full.

Bake until wooden pick inserted in center comes out clean, about 20 minutes. Immediately remove from pan.

NOTE: Recipe can be doubled.

Browned Butter Frosting

⅓ cup margarine or butter	1½ teaspoons vanilla
3 cups powdered sugar	About 2 tablespoons milk

Heat margarine over medium heat until delicate brown; cool. Stir in powdered sugar. Stir in vanilla and milk; beat until frosting is smooth and spreading consistency.

BAKING PAN TIPS

If the recipe makes 36 cupcakes and you have only one 12-cup muffin pan or if you want to make a 3-layer cake and you have only 2 pans, cover and refrigerate the remaining batter while the first cupcakes or layers are baking.

Chocolate Shadow Cupcakes

Chocolate Chip Cupcakes
  (below)
Seven Minute
  Frosting (page 124)

½ ounce melted
  unsweetened
  chocolate
Web, Flower and
  Feather patterns
  (below)

Bake Chocolate Chip Cupcakes as directed. Frost with Seven Minute Frosting and decorate one cupcake at a time. Using a teaspoon, drizzle melted chocolate across frosting in Web, Flower and Feather patterns (see page 124). 1½ dozen cupcakes.

Chocolate Chip Cupcakes

1 egg	1 cup sugar
⅓ cup shortening	1½ teaspoons baking
¾ cup milk	powder
1 teaspoon vanilla	½ teaspoon salt
1¼ cups all-purpose	½ cup semisweet
flour	chocolate chips

Heat oven to 350. Place all ingredients in blender container in order listed. Cover and blend on high speed, stopping blender occasionally to scrape sides, 45 seconds. (Batter will be slightly lumpy.) Pour into paper-lined medium muffin cups, 2½ × 1¼ inches, filling each ⅔ full.

Bake until wooden pick inserted in center comes out clean, 25 to 30 minutes. Immediately remove from pan; cool completely.

Web Pattern

Drizzle circles with chocolate, beginning with small circle in center and encircling with larger circle, ½ inch outside the other. Draw a knife from center outward 8 times, equally spaced.

Flower Pattern

Drizzle circles as for Web. Draw a knife from outside edge inward and from center outward alternately 6 times.

Feather Pattern

Drizzle 3 lines chocolate across frosting; immediately draw a spatula or knife back and fourth across lines.

Big Burger Cake

Yellow Casserole Cake (below)	*Peanut Butter Frosting (right)*
2 teaspoons toasted sesame seed	2 tablespoons cocoa
	1 to 2 tablespoons strawberry preserves

Bake Yellow Casserole Cake as directed. Prepare Peanut Butter Frosting. Cut cake horizontally into 3 equal layers. Frost side only of bottom layer.

Mix ¾ cup of the remaining frosting with the cocoa; if necessary, stir in 1 to 3 teaspoons milk for spreading consistency. Frost top of bottom layer with part of the cocoa frosting. Place middle (hamburger) layer on top; frost top and side of middle layer with remaining cocoa frosting.

Drizzle side of middle layer with preserves to resemble catsup. Place remaining (rounded) layer on top. Frost with remaining frosting. Immediately sprinkle top of cake with toasted sesame seed. 10 to 14 servings.

Yellow Casserole Cake

2 cups all-purpose flour	3 teaspoons baking powder
1 cup sugar	
¼ cup margarine or butter, softened	½ teaspoon salt
	1 teaspoon vanilla
¼ cup shortening	2 eggs
¾ cup milk	

Heat oven to 300°. Grease and flour 1½-quart round glass casserole. Beat all ingredients in large bowl on medium speed, scraping bowl constantly, until blended, about 30 seconds. Beat on high speed, scraping bowl occasionally, 2 minutes. Pour into casserole; spread evenly.

Bake until wooden pick inserted in center comes out clean, 1 hour 5 minutes to 1 hour 15 minutes. Cool 10 minutes; remove from casserole. Cool cake completely.

Peanut Butter Frosting

3 cups powdered sugar	⅓ cup milk
⅓ cup creamy peanut butter	

Beat all ingredients on medium speed until frosting is smooth and spreading consistency. If necessary, stir in additional milk, ½ teaspoon at a time.

NOTE: To toast sesame seed, heat on ungreased cookie sheet in 300° oven until golden brown, about 3 minutes.

○ *Time-saver Tip:* Substitute 1 package (16 ounces) golden pound cake mix for the Yellow Casserole Cake. Prepare and bake as directed on package except use 1½-quart round glass casserole, decrease oven temperature to 300° and bake 1 hour 5 minutes to 1 hour 15 minutes.

Chocolate Gift Loaf

Chocolate Loaf Cake
  (below)
Vanilla Butter Frosting
  (below)

½ package (4 ounces)
  chewy cherry or
  strawberry fruit
  snack

Bake Chocolate Loaf Cake as directed. Frost cake with Vanilla Butter Frosting. Cut sheets of fruit snack into ¾-inch strips. Place strips on frosted cake to resemble wrapped package. For bow, loop strips on top of cake. 14 to 16 servings.

Chocolate Loaf Cake

1½ cups all-purpose
     flour
  1 cup sugar
  ½ cup shortening
  ¾ cup milk
  2 teaspoons baking
     powder

½ teaspoon salt
  1 teaspoon vanilla
  4 egg yolks
  2 ounces melted
     unsweetened
     chocolate (cool)

Heat oven to 350°. Grease and flour loaf pan, 9 × 5 × 3 inches. Beat all ingredients in large bowl on medium speed, scraping bowl constantly, until blended, about 30 seconds. Beat on high speed, scraping bowl occasionally, 3 minutes. Pour into pan.

Bake until wooden pick inserted in center comes out clean, 1 hour 5 minutes to 1 hour 10 minutes. Cool 10 minutes; remove from pan. Cool completely.

Vanilla Butter Frosting

3 cups powdered sugar
⅓ cup margarine or
   butter, softened

1 teaspoon vanilla
1 tablespoon water

Beat all ingredients on medium speed until frosting is smooth and spreading consistency. If necessary, stir in additional water, ½ teaspoon at a time.

Chocolate Gift Loaf

Freezing Cakes

Unfrosted cakes and cupcakes freeze better than frosted cakes. Allow the cakes to cool completely. Place in rigid containers to prevent crushing, then cover with aluminum foil or plastic wrap. Properly packaged, unfrosted cakes can be kept frozen 3 to 4 months. To save time, it's wise to package cake in family portions or single pieces that thaw out quickly.

Of the frosted cakes, those with creamy-type frostings freeze best. Fluffy-type and whipped cream frostings freeze well but tend to stick to the wrapping. To prevent frosting from sticking to the wrapping, freeze cake uncovered 1 hour, insert wooden picks around the top and side of cake, and wrap. Frozen frosted cakes keep for 2 to 3 months.

Gift Cakes

Fluffy White Cake
(below)

Buttercream Frosting
(right)

Bake Fluffy White Cake as directed. Reserve 1½ cups Buttercream Frosting for decorating. Frost cakes with remaining frosting. Tint reserved frosting desired color and decorate as desired. 9 servings each.

Fluffy White Cake

  4 *egg whites*
2¼ *cups all-purpose
     flour or 2½ cups
     cake flour*
1½ *cups sugar*
  ½ *cup shortening (half
     margarine or
     butter, softened)*

2½ *teaspoons baking
     powder*
  1 *teaspoon salt*
1½ *teaspoons vanilla*
  1 *cup milk*

Heat oven to 350°. Grease and flour 2 square foil pans, 7⅞ × 7⅞ × 1¾ inches. Beat egg whites in large bowl until stiff. Beat remaining ingredients except milk in another large bowl on medium speed, scraping bowl constantly, until blended, about 30 seconds.

Beat in milk on medium speed, scraping bowl occasionally, 2 minutes. Fold batter into egg whites. Pour into pans.

Bake until wooden pick inserted in center comes out clean, 30 to 35 minutes. Cool completely.

Buttercream Frosting

4 *cups powdered sugar*
½ *cup margarine or
    butter, softened*
½ *cup shortening*

1 *teaspoon almond
    extract*
3 *tablespoons milk*

Beat all ingredients on medium speed until frosting is smooth and of spreading consistency. If necessary, stir in additional milk, 1 teaspoon at a time.

Flower Cupcakes

*Starlight Cupcakes
 (page 71)
 or Chocolate Cupcakes
 (page 150)*

*Buttercream Decorator
 Frosting (below)
 Red, yellow and green
 food color*

Bake Starlight Cupcakes as directed. Frost half of the cupcakes with thin coat of Buttercream Decorator Frosting (use the remaining cupcakes as desired). Tint remaining frosting desired color (see below). Holding cupcake in one hand, pipe desired flower onto each cupcake (see below and page 10). 1½ dozen cupcakes.

Suggestions:

For 4 roses, tint 1 cup frosting pink with 3 or 4 drops red food color. Use petal tip #124.

For 4 marigolds, tint 1 cup frosting yellow with 3 or 4 drops yellow food color. Use petal tip #104. Use any remaining yellow frosting for stamens of wild roses.

For 20 violets, tint ½ cup frosting violet with paste food color. Pipe 3 to 5 violets onto each cupcake (see page 44).

For 9 to 12 wild roses, tint ¾ cup frosting pale pink with 1 or 2 drops red food color.

For leaves, tint ¼ cup frosting green with 1 drop green food color. Use leaf tip #352.

Buttercream Decorator Frosting

*6 cups powdered sugar
¾ cup margarine or
 butter, softened
¾ cup shortening*

*3 tablespoons water
1½ teaspoons almond
 extract*

Beat all ingredients on medium speed until frosting is smooth and desired consistency. If necessary, stir in additional powdered sugar. (Roses may need additional powdered sugar.)

○ *Time-saver Tip:* Substitute 1 package (18.5 ounces) yellow cake mix with pudding for the Yellow Cupcakes. Prepare and bake as directed on package for cupcakes.

Flower Cupcakes

Glazed Fruitcake

Whole Wheat Fruitcake
(below)

Apple Jelly Glaze (below)
Creamy Frosting (below)

Bake Whole Wheat Fruitcake as directed. Spread with Apple Jelly Glaze and decorate with almonds or frost with Creamy Frosting and decorate with candied fruit if desired. 2 loaves.

Whole Wheat Fruitcake

1½ cups whole wheat flour	15 ounces golden raisins (about 3 cups)
1½ cups all-purpose flour	12 ounces candied pineapple, cut up (about 2 cups)
1¼ cups sugar	
¾ cup margarine or butter, softened	4 ounces candied citron, cut up (about ⅔ cup)
¾ cup shortening	
⅔ cup orange juice	4 ounces candied orange peel, cut up (about ⅔ cup)
1½ teaspoons baking powder	
¾ teaspoon salt	¾ cup flaked coconut
9 eggs	8 ounces blanched whole almonds (about 1½ cups)
16 ounces candied cherries, cut into halves (about 2½ cups)	
	8 ounces pecan halves (about 2 cups)

Heat oven to 275°. Line 2 loaf pans, 9 × 5 × 3 inches, with aluminum foil; grease. Beat flours, sugar, margarine, shortening, orange juice, baking powder, salt and eggs in large bowl on medium speed, scraping bowl constantly, until blended, about 30 seconds. Beat on high speed, scraping bowl occasionally, 3 minutes. Mix batter into fruits and nuts in 6-quart bowl. Spread mixture in pans.

Bake until wooden pick inserted in center comes out clean, 2½ to 3 hours. Remove from pans; cool.

Apple Jelly Glaze

Heat ¼ cup apple jelly over low heat until melted.

Creamy Frosting

⅓ cup margarine or butter	1½ teaspoons vanilla
2 cups powdered sugar	2 to 4 tablespoons hot water

Heat margarine in saucepan until melted. Stir in powdered sugar and vanilla. Stir in water, 1 tablespoon at a time, until frosting is desired consistency.

Fruitcake Ring

Mincemeat Fruitcake
(below)
Browned Butter Glaze
(below)

⅓ cup coarsely chopped pecans

Bake Mincemeat Fruitcake as directed. Spread with Browned Butter Glaze, letting it run down side unevenly. Immediately sprinkle top with pecans.

Mincemeat Fruitcake

2 eggs	1 can (14 ounces) sweetened condensed milk
1 jar (28 ounces) ready-to-use mincemeat	
	1 cup coarsely chopped pecans
16 ounces mixed candied fruit (about 2 cups)	2½ cups all-purpose flour
	1 teaspoon baking soda

Heat oven to 300°. Generously grease and flour 12-cup bundt cake pan or tube pan, 10 × 4 inches. Beat eggs slightly in large bowl. Stir in mincemeat, candied fruit, sweetened condensed milk and pecans. Stir in flour and baking soda. Pour batter into pan.

Bake until wooden pick inserted in center comes out clean, about 1 hour 50 minutes. Cool 15 minutes; remove from pan. Cool completely.

Browned Butter Glaze

2 tablespoons margarine or butter	1 teaspoon vanilla
1 cup powdered sugar	1 tablespoon hot water

Heat margarine in saucepan over medium heat until delicate brown. Cool slightly. Stir in powdered sugar, vanilla and water. If necessary, stir in additional hot water, 1 teaspoon at a time, until glaze is desired consistency.

Cutting Cakes

Use a sharp, thin knife to cut shortening-type cakes, a long serrated knife for angels and chiffons. If the frosting sticks, dip the knife into hot water and wipe with a damp paper towel after cutting each slice.

Fruitcake Ring, top, Glazed Fruitcake, bottom

Index